Mexican Cities of the Gods

MEXICAN CITIES OF THE GODS

An Archaeological Guide

HANS HELFRITZ

FREDERICK A. PRAEGER, *Publishers*

New York · Washington · London

Frederick A. Praeger, *Publishers*
111 Fourth Avenue, New York, N.Y. 10003, U.S.A.
5, Cromwell Place, London S.W.7, England

Published in the United States of America in 1970
by Frederick A. Praeger, Inc., Publishers

© 1968 by Verlag M. DuMont Schauberg, Köln

Library of Congress Catalog Card Number: 75-85518

Printed in West Germany

Contents

Landscape and Environment of the Ancient Mexicans 7

I Religious Monuments of the Plateau 11

    1 Cuicuilco 14
    2 Teotihuacán 16
    3 Tula (Tollán) 39
    4 Tenayuca and Santa Cecilia 43
    5 Calixtlahuaca 46
    6 Malinalco 48
    7 Xochicalco 50

II Religious Monuments of the Gulf Coast 53

    8 La Venta, Tres Zapotes and Cerro de las Mesas 54
    9 El Tajín 65

III Religious Monuments of the South 69

    10 Monte Albán 70
    11 Mitla 75

    THE MAYA 79

    12 Palenque 133
    13 Sayil – Labná – Kabáh 140
    14 Uxmal 147
    15 Chichén-Itzá 152

Advice on Travelling in Mexico 161

Bibliography 178

Index 179

Pronunciation Guide

Pronunciation of proper nouns generally follows the rules of Spanish. Words ending in a vowel or 'n' or 's' have the stress on the penultimate syllable. Exceptions to this rule are indicated by an accent. Words ending in a consonant other than 'n' and 's' are stressed on the last syllable.

'X' at the beginning of a word is pronounced 'sh'. If it comes in the middle of a word, as in 'México', it is pronounced like a strong 'h'.

'J' is pronounced like a strongly aspirated 'h'.

'Z' is pronounced like 's'.

'C' before 'e' and 'i' is soft, but otherwise hard.

'Ll' is pronounced like 'ly' and 'ñ' like 'ny'.

Landscape and Environment of the Ancient Mexicans

The landscape, climate and nature of the soil have all affected the character of early Mexican architecture. The jungle and the endless expanse of the plateau gave the ancient Mexicans a distinctive feeling for space. The harmony between buildings and landscape is the main element in their great art and the reason why it seems so close to our own ideas today. The imposing effect of this architecture is heightened by the beautifully carved ornamentation and the colouring, which are also strongly influenced by the landscape.

There has been virtually no other people from any of the ancient civilisations either in Europe or Asia who could so transform a piece of nature by piling up and excavating the soil. In this way the Mexicans were able to produce not just one, but a whole series of temple precincts with raised platforms, sunken squares and pyramids such as marked the centres of their city-states in their former splendour. The amount of effort needed for this transformation of nature depended on the topography of the site, and varies according to the landscape and the town.

There was very rarely any miltary purpose behind the design of these gigantic constructions, probably only in the case of those buildings set up on high points at Monte Albán and Xochicalco, which seem to hang above deep valleys and are wonderfully impressive. Generally speaking the complexes of buildings which the architects of various Middle American or Central American civilisations erected must be regarded as the focal point of their religious and ceremonial life. Sloping terraces and stairways are the main features of ancient Mexican architecture, and occur over and over again as a means of defining space. They form the links between platforms at various levels and were used in the religious ceremonial of sacrifices which, particularly among the Aztecs, took such a gruesome form.

Even in those sites which were laid out as defensive strongholds the spaces between the buildings also served as places for public ceremonies.

Priests controlled the fate of these peoples, and it was only a combination of religious belief and a readiness for self-sacrifice caused by spiritual necessity which made it possible to build these religious monuments, whose original splendour, judging by what remains today, can hardly be imagined. They could be compared to Delphi or Olympia in ancient Greece, since they represent the centres of spiritual life of the various Indian nations. They are different, however, in that their influence did not extend above and beyond the political boundaries, as with their Greek counterparts. They were monumental symbols of the power of particular deities and the politically independent peoples who worshipped them. Religious observances maintained a feeling of unity among individual nations. The communities would come together in assemblies at these temple complexes under the guidance of an exalted priesthood.

While religious life was centred round these places, the ordinary members of the community lived in widely-scattered settlements, generally no more than villages. In wooded areas especially, where it was continually necessary to clear fresh ground for agriculture, there were no permanent towns as we understand them.

The Indians' huts were built of perishable materials, as they are in many parts of Mexico to this day. The method of house-building among the Indians of Yucatán, for example, has not changed at all since the time of their ancestors. The huts projecting out in front of the magnificent Labná Gate provide an attractive example of this. It was as necessary to level the ground when building a simple hut as it was for the construction of a temple or a ceremonial square. We can see from the lay-out of such levelled areas, where they have survived, that just like the large-scale public squares with a definite religious purpose, the spaces between the dwellings were an important part of the relation of one building to another. However, the real discoveries of the last 150 years – the history of discovery in Middle America hardly reaches back beyond this point – are not the remains of dwelling-places, but stone monuments of the temple-cities of the Maya and the creators of the Teotihuacán Culture who built the giant temples of the sun and moon and the sanctuary of Quetzalcoatl with its decoration of reliefs. They are the recently discovered sites of Tula, or Tollán as it was known in the time of the Toltecs, and the few buildings of the Aztecs, whose capital city, Tenochtitlán, with all its palaces, pyramids and temples was destroyed after the arrival of the Spanish conquerors.

The ancient Mexicans dedicated their great buildings to the gods. They made a wonderfully solemn background for the ritual which occupied a dominant place in the communal life of all ancient Mexican cultures. What is more, the people who created these temples and pyramids, the sacrificial bowls and calendar-stones, the frieze of brilliant white limestone mosaics and reddish-coloured faces of the Atlantes of Tula, have not died out. They still live on in the Indian villages of Yucatán and the thatched mud-huts in the shade of organ cacti on the Mexican Plateau.

The strong communal sense which the structure of the ancient city-state produced also still exists among the Mexican people. No country in the world has such ancient traditions and so many remains of its great past as Mexico. There are no less than 11,000 archaeological sites in the care of the Instituto Nacional de Antropología e Historia. More than 3000 of these are medium-sized or larger settlements, yet less than one tenth of them has been archaeologically investigated. However, we can be sure that finds uncovered on Mexican soil and the architectural masterpieces discovered here represent a high level of artistic achievement, and are equal in quality to any of the ancient civilisations of the Old World.

When in 1906 painters like Picasso and Matisse first introduced the art of the African negro into the salons of European art-lovers, a general reappraisal of artistic judgement began. The idea of "art" inherited from the Greeks, which until then had been taken as the yardstick of artistic value, began to be disregarded. Suddenly the great power of expression in works of ancient Mexican art was recognised, and it was realised that the roots of this art lay in world of religion.

The sculpture which the Mexican "artist" created – though in fact the idea of "art" in our sense never existed among any of the ancient American peoples – was not a portrayal of a supernatural being, but a symbol. Just as a great many African carved figures are believed to be occasionally or permanently inhabited by souls, and the consecration of a statue in ancient Egypt or Babylon made it a potent source of power and filled it with spiritual life, so the images of Mexican gods had souls, and the whole of nature as they saw it possessed feelings and emotions.

Architecture and the planning of towns both depended on the fundamental element of Mexican life: religion. It was Mathematics and Astronomy, both of which were closely linked to religion and reached their highest development in the Mexican calendar, which made it possible to build these architectural masterpieces with such a confident feeling for style.

All the cultures of ancient Mexico show common traits, although they developed in different areas during different periods. Nevertheless, within this general line of development there are characteristic variations in religious and social ideas as well as in art and architecture.

I Religious Monuments of the Plateau

Archaic cultures 1500 - 100 B.C.
Teotihuacán culture 200 B.C. - A.D. 900
Toltecs of Tollán A.D. 900 - 1168
Aztec culture A.D. 1324 - 1521

Mexico is a land of Indians even today. All one has to do to realise this is visit the ruins of Teotihuacán or Chichén-Itzá on a public holiday. The ordinary folk who are still Indians, wander about among the ruins showing a lively interest in everything. They follow the latest excavations and express deep admiration for the works of art of their Indian ancestors.

Who are these Indians and where do they come from? Archaeologists are now fairly sure that America was settled by migrations across the Bering Strait or the Aleutians. They came by foot, as there was a continuous land-bridge across the Bering Strait during the Ice Age linking America and Asia. At the end of the Ice Age the level of the oceans rose considerably, and the bridge sank below the sea. The theory of migration across the Bering Strait is the only one as yet with any scientific evidence behind it. There is no evidence that man evolved independently on the continent of America.

It has been calculated from the results of recent finds that men were living in the region now occupied by Mexico about 20,000 years ago. We must assume that men arrived from Asia in relatively small groups and over long periods of time. The first to arrive must have crossed the huge glaciers of the Bering Strait and then made their way towards the ice-free south. Until the end of the Ice Age and even for a short time afterwards there were mammoths, the mastodon, the giant elephant and vast herds of camels and wild horses living in America. In one find at Tequixquiác, north-west of Mexico City, crude man-made tools have been discovered together with the remains of bones from forms of animal life that flourished in the Ice Age, which may be about 28,000 years old. This was a tremendous discovery, but there are still many gaps in the story of man's arrival in America. First of all there must be a clear system of dating for the whole of American pre-history. There are anthropological and cultural problems too. Why did the development of civilised cultures take place in limited areas of America a few thousand years later than in the Old World? How did the discrepancy in the pace of development arise? Differences in environment certainly have a part to play. Probably there are also differences in the capacity to develop between the various races of *homo sapiens*. All these problems arise when we attempt to trace the first inhabitants of America. We are still looking for the "oldest American".

8000 years ago nomadic tribes of hunters and gatherers of plants, still streamed down from the north. Archaeologists find a great deal of material in the "hunters' bone-yards" and huge waste-heaps, which helps them throw some light on the history of man in America. In this way we can follow the progress of Asiatic tribes down to Tierra del Fuego. These tribes were the first inhabitants of America.

The Archaic Period in Mexico, according to studies undertaken with carbon-14 dating, begins in the second millenium, or in some places the third millenium, B. C. This is the time of the first farmers. The first example of craftsmanship does not appear until 1000 B.C., in the form of attractive pottery. The most productive site where this has been found is Tlatilco at Atzcapotzalco, now within the limits of Mexico City. The numerous clay figurines of graceful dancing women with elaborately coiffed hair, small breasts and rich jewelry represent a distinct style, which archaeologists call "pretty ladies".

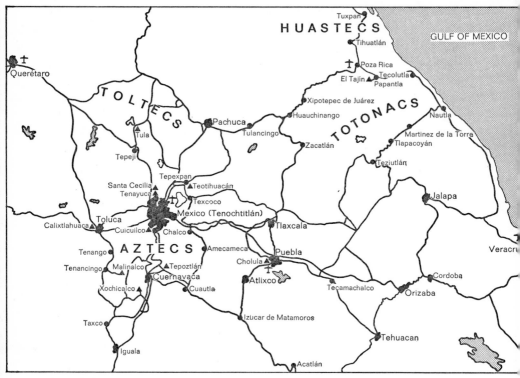

HUASTECS

Tuxpan

Tihuatlán

GULF OF MEXICO

Querétaro

Poza Rica

El Tajín ▲ Tecolutla
Papantla

TOLTECS

Xipotepec de Juárez

Pachuca

Huauchinango

TOTONACS

Nautla

Tula

Tulancingo

Zacatlán

Martinez de la Torre

Tlapacoyán

Tepeji

Teziutlán

Tepexpan

Santa Cecilia

Tenayuca

Teotihuacán

Jalapa

Texcoco

Mexico (Tenochtitlán)

Toluca

Calixtlahuaca

Cuicuilco

Chalco

Tlaxcala

Tenango

AZTECS

Amecameca

Puebla

Veracruz

Tenancingo

Malinalco

Tepoztlán

Cholula

Xochicalco

Cuernavaca

Atlixco

Córdoba

Cuautla

Tecamachalco

Orizaba

Taxco

Izucar de Matamoros

Tehuacan

Iguala

Acatlán

Central Plateau of Mexico. Region of the archaic peoples, Toltecs and Aztecs

1 Cuicuilco

The first signs of building also appear in the archaic levels. The oldest example of this in central highland Mexico is the Pyramid of Cuicuilco. We may perhaps one day find more remains from the Archaic Period, but most of the buildings of this time must be lost for ever. The Pyramid of Cuicuilco was encased up to a third of its height in lava overflowing from the volcano Xitle. The date when this happened is not known, but was probably some time before the birth of Christ. This lava stream, now set as hard as iron, forms the so-called Pedregal on the southern edge of Mexico City, and the new University of Mexico has been built on it. All the basic elements of classic Indian pyramid design are already present.

The custom of building a temple on an "artificial mountain" is found all over Middle America. The original form was an artificial mound which was rounded like a real hill. This was covered with a layer of stones and later became square in shape so that the form of a flat-topped pyramid arose. Because of the picture of the Universe which the builders had, it was also to some extent a "symbol of the heavens" in Walter Krickeberg's opinion, for "while we regard the sky as a dome, other races see it as a mountain which the sun climbs up in the morning and descends in the afternoon, and its slopes are therefore like steps on a gigantic building".

The Pyramid of Cuicuilco is an almost round truncated cone about 65ft in height. It is now, after the difficult task of excavation – the hill was, like so many other pyramid sites, completely overgrown with undergrowth and cacti – between 25 and 40ft less than its original height. Its original diameter was about 400ft. There are four rows of steps and a platform, on which the temple once stood, built on top of the round base. There is a rough stairway on the east side, and a ramp and three flights of stairs on the west side led up to the raised altar. In later times the pyramid-steps were always linked with the numbers 9 and 13, representing the "nine lords of the underworld" and the "thirteen lords of the day".

Cuicuilco means in the Nahuatl language "place of singing and dancing". We could well call it the "Mexican Pompeii" because not far from the pyramid, at a place called Copilco, remains of settlements and burial-grounds have been uncovered under the 30 square mile lava-field of the Pedregal. Just as at Pompeii, the volcanic eruption must have caught the inhabitants completely by surprise because the imprints of men and dogs were unable to escape have been found in the solidified lava. These and other discoveries have shown that the archaic people of the Copilco-Cuicuilco Period cultivated maize, caught fish in the lakes, kept dogs and used quartz and obsidian arrow-heads. Ornaments of jade and sea-shells suggest that they also traded with other peoples.

2 Teotihuacán

When the Spaniards conquered Mexico at the beginning of the 16th century they also went to Teotihuacán, but no-one could tell them anything about the builders of the Pyramids of the Sun and Moon. The Aztecs believed they must have been a race of giants to erect such colossal monuments, and to prove it they showed the Spaniards giant thigh-bones. These, however, were not human but came from the giant elephant which still lived in Mexico in the Diluvian Period, and grew to a height of 16ft. And what do we know about the builders of Teotihuacán? Basically not much more than that they were not Aztecs.

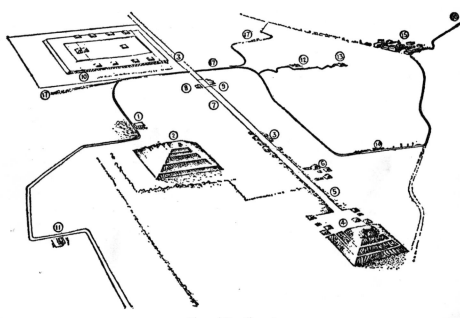

Plan of Teotihuacán

1 Museum
2 Pyramid of the Sun
3 Way of the Dead
4 Pyramid of the Moon
5 Temple of the fertility gods
6 Square with pillars
7 Building with mica slabs
8 Temple of Tlaloc
9 Underground chambers

10 The so-called Citadel with the temple of Quetzalcoatl
11 Tepantitla
12 Tetitla
13 Atetelco
14 The 'Copper House'
15 San Juan de Teotihuacán village
16 Road to Mexico
17 San Juan River

The metroplis had probably already been in ruins for two or three hundred years at that time. Charred beams found under the remains of many houses have been tested with carbon-14 dating, and have shown that the collapse of the city took place in the 8th century, presumably caused by a great fire. The memory of the Teotihuacán civilisation lived on in Aztec tradition, but was lost in myth. In any case, the roots of this culture must go back deep into archaic times.

The name Teotihuacán is an Aztec word meaning "the place where one becomes a god". The famous and learned Franciscan monk Bernárdino de Sahagún (1499-1590), the historian of pre-Spanish cultures, explains the name in the following way: ". . . and they called the place Teotihuacán because it was the burial-place of kings. The ancients said that when a man died, he had become a god, and so that came to mean that he had died."

Although the semi-mythical prehistory of the people who built the most colossal monuments of the Mexican Plateau is lost in the darkness of the Archaic, that is, pre-classical, Period, archaeologists still refer to them as "classic" in recognition of their astonishing achievements in architecture and craftsmanship.

The culture of Teotihuacán is generally divided into four periods. The first two are still Archaic. At this time construction of the two great pyramids began, but the pottery was very primitive. The third, or Classic period lies between A.D. 300 and A.D. 600, and marks the apogee of Teotihuacán culture. The town covered an area of over 4 square miles and it is believed that about 85,000 people lived there. The destruction of the city occurred in the fourth period. At first the inhabitants abandoned it entirely, yet somehow the culture continued to develop. During the next two hundred years part of the population returned, apparently to protect the treasures. Remains of pottery from this period discovered in waste-pits show that these people were closely related to the original inhabitants.

During this stage, which did not end until about the year 1000, pottery and painting reached their zenith.

Teotihuacán, the great Classic centre of Middle America, must certainly have been ruled by a caste of priests. The most important buildings of the ceremonial centre were intended for religious purposes, and the houses round this area were occupied by the ruling priesthood.

The town stands quite open and exposed in the landscape. No trace of fortification has been found. On the other hand Teotihuacán must have had extensive trade-relations from the beginning. Its cultural and artistic influence can be traced beyond Monte Albán as far south as the peninsula of Yucatán and Guatemala.

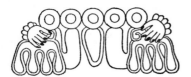

Hand motif in Teotihuacán.
The downward-hanging
shapes symbolise hearts

The divine hand, chief
motif of a fresco in
Teotihuacán

Just recently a stone slab bearing a relief of the Teotihuacán rain-god was found in Tikal, and at Kaminaljuyú, close to the boundaries of Guatemala City, a pyramid has been uncovered which shows the typical features of the Moon Pyramid at Teotihuacán. There are particularly close parallels in the pottery. In Kaminaljuyú three-legged pots of pure Teotihuacán design have been found which definitely came originally from Teotihuacán. The decoration in the Maya style using the "stucco technique" was added later. The striking influence of Teotihuacán in the Mayan region is also very clearly seen in the architecture of the Esperanza Phase at Kaminaljuyú.

Teotihuacán was built to honour the gods. It was a city of the gods "where buried kings became gods", but it was in no sense a city of the dead as the Aztecs thought. It was one of the few places in Middle America where human dwellings were closely connected with sacred buildings. Above all, it was a magnificent temple-city pulsating with life. Today it is the most imposing and popular of the ancient Mexican cities. Lying at an altitude of 7500ft, it is only a 25 miles as the crow flies from Mexico City across the almost treeless high plateau of Anahuác. The Sun Pyramid stands at the centre of a vast precinct, and is larger in volume than the pyramid of Cheops in Egypt. With a height of 215ft and a base 725ft square, it contains about a million tons of sun-dried mud bricks. This massive structure is an amazing sight, especially as one must remember that the priest-kings who built it had no modern aids at their disposal. They did not have the wheel and they had no draught animals. The rulers must have had an incredible degree of power to be able to make their subjects literally "move mountains". Even so, what we see of the Sun Pyramid today, in spite of all the reconstruction and restoration done when the site was excavated, is incomplete and in some ways misleading. For one thing the temple which crowned the topmost platform is missing.

Section of the mural at Tepantitla-Teotihuacán showing the Paradise of Tlaloc. The figures are dancing and singing, playing ball, catching butterflies and picking flowers

There used to be a layer of stucco several feet thick and painted in brilliant colours covering the stone facing, which is now exposed. The pyramid must have presented a much livelier appearance in early times than it does today. It has a larger base than any other pyramid of either the Old or the New Worlds, and yet it is not the biggest in Mexico. The Pyramid of Cholula, now under excavation is the largest in the New World. The site was continuously occupied from the Preclassic Period to the Spanish Conquest.

One noticeable thing about the Sun Pyramid is the unequal height of the levels and the way their sides slope at different angles. To the left and right of a kind of podium built out in front there is a stairway leading up to the platform on top. The stairway goes up to the first level in two separate arms angled inwards toward one another. The two arms then lead up to the third level, and finally one single stairway leads to the fourth and fifth and topmost platform. Between 1920 and 1930 two tunnels were driven through the pyramid, and this revealed that it had been designed and built from the beginning in its present form. There had been no second structure built over the first, as has been found with many pyramids.

The great long axis which cuts through the ceremonial centre of the city was called the "Way of the Dead" by the Aztecs. The name originated with them, and reflects their spiritual outlook. However this is not necessarily the same as that of the people of Teotihuacán. The "Sun Pyramid" was actually not dedicated to the sun at all, but should probably be thought of as the temple of a fire-god or a water-god. The so-called Way of the Dead is an absolutely straight road which begins in the south by the little Río San Juán and ends in the steps of the Moon Pyramid just over a mile to the north. They seem to lead upwards into the heavens like Jacob's ladder. The Way of the Dead is flanked on the east by the Sun Pyramid and the so-called "Citadel", which is now believed to have been the centre of the city. The centre was also marked by avenues cutting the Way of the Dead at right angles. The lay-out of all the sacred buildings of Teotihuacán is related to this axis.

The height of the Moon Pyramid, at 140ft, corresponds exactly with that of the Sun Pyramid, as it stands on somewhat higher ground. The Aztecs believed that a stone figure 10ft high and weighing 22 tons had formerly stood on this pyramid and that this was a moon idol. It was in fact later found near the Moon Pyramid, but is probably a statue of a water-goddess.

It is quite incorrect to call the complex of 15 pyramid bases a "citadel". These remains surround an inner court with sides more than 400 yards long. There is no doubt that it is a temple-site rather than any sort of fortification.

d 2

Pyramid of Cuicuilco, an
ost round truncated cone
eet high, is the oldest
wn pyramid in central
land Mexico. It was en-
d in an outflow of lava
the volcano Xitle up to
third of its height before
Christian Era

3 The so-called 'Citadel' with the main temple of Quetzalcoatl in Teotihuacán

4 The 215 feet high Sun Pyramid of Teotihuacán which is greater in volume than the Pyramid of Cheops

tone sculpture of the Aztec earth-goddess Coatlicue 8 feet high

6 One of the 15 feet high 'Atlantes' and two pillars which once supported the roof of the temple or Pyramid of Tula (Tollán)

illars of the ante-chamber and the five-stepped main pyramid of Tula

ead of one of the 'Atlantes' which represent arriors and in an extended sense, Quetzalcoatl

9   Figure of a warrior on a pilaster

Bas-relief of an eagle swallowing a heart from the Temple of Venus at Tula

Chac Mool, the messenger of the gods, with a sacrifical bowl cut out of the stone on his chest. Tula

Bas-relief of a jaguar from the Temple of Venus at Tula. The jaguar symbolises a Toltec warrior

Frieze with snakes swallowing skeletons with half their flesh removed on the frieze of the Coatepantli

14 The Aztec Serpent-Pyramid of Tenayuca

15 One of the two coiled stone 'fire serpents'

16 Stone snakes at the foot of the pyramid of Tenayuca

17 The temple-pyramid of Santa Cecilia. The only Aztec pyramid whose temple has survived

18 The round pyramid of Calixtlahuaca dedicated to Quetzalcoatl as the Wind God

19 Raised platforms and skull-rack in Calixtlahuaca

20   The temple of Malinalco carved out of the cliff-face. On either side of the stairway there are stone jag
also carved from the living rock

21 The main temple-pyramid of Xochicalco with a relief-frieze on its base

22 Warrior sitting cross-legged with shield and spears and symbolic signs on the base of the temple on the pyramid of Xochicalco

24 and 25
Priest sitting cross-legged
Quetzalcoatl as the plumed serp
on the frieze on the base of
temple-pyramid of Xochicalco

◁ 23   Ball-court with sloping playing area and stone rings in Xochicalco

The most impressive building of all is the main temple, which the Aztecs believed to be dedicated to the plumed serpent Quetzalcoatl. It has six levels which diminish in height towards the top. These are decorated with horizontal squared cornices and high reliefs of plumed serpents and masks of demonic beings, which have survived in good condition. On the bottom edges there are low reliefs of writhing serpent bodies. Images of shells and all kinds of sea

The cross of the five areas of the world with their gods. In the middle stands the god of fire, who lives in the 'navel of the Earth'. There are two gods placed at the ends of the Earth in each of the four directions as lords and protectors. In between, the symbols for the days of the calendar have been reproduced

creatures complete this unique design. Traces of painting show that here, too, the combination of colour and form had been used to make a tremendous impression on the observer. There is no doubt that the plumed serpent on this temple is supposed to represent some divine being.

The plumed serpent called Quetzalcoatl by the Aztecs was also an important deity possessing a variety of different roles among other cultures. For example, the deity shown in this magnificent temple-decoration is undoubtedly closely related to the water-god. This is clear from the images. Just as the rain-god Tlaloc was the most honoured god of the Aztecs, so the rain-god was certainly the highest being in the Teotihuacán pantheon. Krickeberg believes the plumed serpent portrayed on the façade of the central temple in the "Citadel" to be an "embodiment of the waters of the world", because it is surrounded by sea-shells.

There were two other gods in Teotihuacán who came next in rank to the water-god: the fire-god and the "fat god". We know the fire-god from many portrayals in stone and pottery, which show him as an old man in a sitting position with a bowl of fire on his back. The "fat god" is thought to have been rather like the Chinese god of good fortune. Pottery figurines of him are frequently found.

One of the most splendid buildings at Teotihuacán is the Palace of Quetzal-papalotl (the Butterfly-Bird, whose motif is found on the columns of the western square). It contains painted frescoes, well-preserved roof combs and elaborately designed complexes of chambers.

Hieroglyph of the city of Tollán. The name means 'place of the bulrush' or 'reed-city' in the Nahuatl language

3   *Tula (Tollán)*

Around the year A.D. 900 a new wave of wild hordes pressed down from the north on to the Mexican Plateau. They mixed with the races already living there, adopted their civilisation, founded a capital city called Tollán and called themselves from then on Toltecs. Their art, which was as firmly rooted in the world of the gods as that of Teotihuacán, clearly expresses the Toltecs' concern with military power. This epoch, beginning with the semi-mythical conqueror Mixcoatl, is known as the Early Post-Classic Period.

The spiritual world of the ancient Mexicans underwent a complete transformation, bringing about an entirely new outlook on life. The Toltecs believed they were living in the age of the "Fifth Sun". All four previous mythical ages had been created by the gods and had ended in a great natural catastrophe. The first age of the universe had ended with an invasion of pitch-black darkness. The second ended with terrible whirlwinds, the third with a fire-storm, and the world of the fourth age was destroyed by a great deluge. The "Fifth Sun", which is the one we are living under, would be destroyed too, but this time by an earthquake.

The lives of the ancient Mexicans must have been darkened by a constant shadow of unimaginable terror that the sun might disappear. There was just one thing which could delay, though not prevent, this catastrophe: human sacrifice, for human blood and the human heart were the most precious things that could be offered to the gods.

While the Toltecs still kept the number of human sacrifices within limits, the Aztecs raised the numbers to an incredible level. The insatiable new gods of the heavens, above all the Sun God, demanded blood – and blood could only be provided by the sacrifice of prisoners taken in war.

The changes in beliefs and religious practices were accompanied by changes in art, particularly in the handling of motifs. Temple walls were decorated with reliefs of warlike figures, jaguars and serpents swallowing human hearts. There are also new architectural ideas which appeared at this time. Pillars were used, and this meant a new sense of space. Pilasters, columns and Atlantes produce the overwhelming impressiveness of Tollán, the former capital and temple-city of the Toltecs.

The ruins of Tollán are situated very close to the Mexican town of Tula in the state of Hidalgo, about 50 miles from Mexico City. Even as late as the thirties it was widely doubted that these ruins could really be the ancient city of Tollán. When the Mexican archaeologist J. R. Acosta first began to dig there in 1940 restoring the totally destroyed city seemed an impossible task. As at Teotihuacán, there is a residential area and a ceremonial centre, though this is considerably smaller than the one at Teotihuacán. The west axis runs at 17 degrees from the parallel to face the point at which the sun sets after reaching its zenith twice a year.

The name Tollán means in Nahuatl "city of rushes" or simply "capital city". It is overshadowed by a large temple-pyramid built in five steps. This differs noticeably from the ones at Teotihuacán because of the great breadth of its platform. The whole of this spacious surface area was formerly taken up by the temple. As the outside walls could not support such a large roof on their own, free-standing supports were devised as an additional means of taking the weight. The pillars and columns were decorated with reliefs and the four massive supports of the front row carved into colossal statues of war-like figures 15 ft high.

The roof of the ante-chamber is supported by two round columns in the shape of plumed serpents. The Atlantes, as the colossal statues of warriors are called, wear butterfly-shaped breast-plates in the form of reliefs. Each figure has a sling in its right hand and a bag of copal, or incense, and a dart and spear-thrower in the left. The hollows of their eyes and mouths were originally inlaid with precious stones, and their faces were painted. These warriors represent Quetzalcoatl in a different role. Here he is in his alternative identity as Tlahuiz-calpantecuhtli or "Morning Star". The pyramid is named the "Temple of the Morning Star" (or "Temple of Venus") because of these stone figures.

The Coatepantli, which adjoins this building, has a wall 130 ft long and seven feet high. This is decorated with a frieze of reliefs showing snakes swallowing skeletons with half their flesh removed.

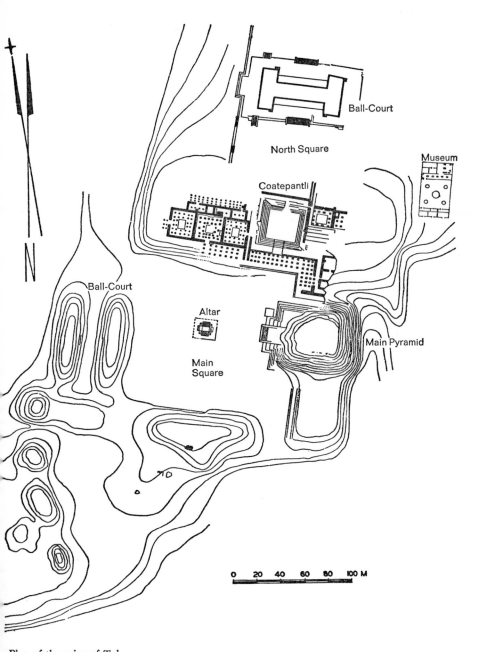

N

Ball-Court

North Square

Coatepantli

Museum

Ball-Court

Altar

Main
Square

Main Pyramid

0   20   40   60   80   100 M

Plan of the ruins of Tula

The tremendous impression which this temple-city makes comes from its columns and pillars, and the Atlantes. Like a phoenix rising from the ashes, it was reconstructed from a great mass of rubble. The Atlantes were laboriously rebuilt from many fragments scattered about among the debris and replaced on the pyramid platform where they had once supported the temple roof. We cannot be sure that the fragments of masonry, the monolithic blocks of the columns and the many reliefs have been assembled exactly as they were, but the present arrangement is certainly impressive.

Quetzalcoatl was a half-mythical figure in the kingdom of the Toltecs. His original name was Ce Acatl (One Reed) Topiltzin (Our Prince). He was the foremost spiritual and temporal Toltec leader and like many other priest-kings, he took the name of the highest god, Quetzalcoatl. He is supposed to have lived for 52 years, from A.D. 947 to 999, according to the chronicles. Ce Acatl Quetzalcoatl appears to have been overthrown by his opponents, but he disappears in a baffling confusion of historical fact and myth. According to one version, he travelled to Yucatán with his following and was received with honour by the Mayas. This is believed to be the time when the artistic and architectural traditions of the Toltecs and the Mayans were merged. In another legend he went to the "Land of Black and Red Colours", where he was supposed to have burned himself. His heart became the morning star.

Toltecs continued to rule in Tollán for about 200 years. In 1168 another wave of hostile hordes called the Chichimecs invaded the region and completely destroyed the city. This sealed the fate of the once-powerful kingdom. Quetzalcoatl's appearance and disappearance on earth heralded an age which centuries later came to be ruled by bloodthirsty gods and was to end in horrible wars.

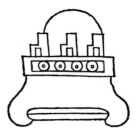

Hieroglyph of the city of Tenayuca. The name comes from the Aztec words *tenamitl* (rampart) and the suffix *yancoc* (place), and means the fortified place

4 Tenayuca and Santa Cecilia

The era of peace glorified in old sagas was over. A powerful caste of warriors and traders came to the fore. Conflict between the priesthood and the warriors grew up, the results of which are described in many myths. The Aztecs had a blood-thirsty counterpart to the peaceable Quetzalcoatl in Tezcatlipoca, the god with the "smoking mirror". The myth of the god-king Quetzalcoatl continued to live on among the people. When Hernando Cortés came across the Atlantic in 1519, this must certainly have hastened their downfall. They took Cortés to be the god risen again, and threw caution to the winds. They must have been bitterly disappointed, for not only was the great empire of the Aztecs destroyed, but all their wonderful buildings with it. There is virtually nothing left of the ancient capital, Tenochtitlán. Even though the reports of the Spaniards are full of admiration for the palaces, temples and pyramids of this city, they destroyed it utterly and built the new capital, Mexico, on its ruins.

Only a few foundations now remain. We know from drawings and descriptions, although these are not at all accurate, that the most important building of Tenochtitlán, which is thought to have had a population of between 30,000

Tezcatlipoca in turkey costume. He had many different roles. He was the personification of the night sky, the winter and the north

and 75,000 at one time, was a huge double pyramid with temples to Tlaloc the Rain-God and Huitzilopochtli, the God of War or the "Mexican Mars". This was the scene of terrible human sacrifices in the time just before the Spanish conquest. We can form an idea of what it looked like from the Pyramid of Tenayuca, which has survived in good condition and been well restored, though it is much smaller.

This pyramid was a provincial religious monument not far from the capital. It was first built a long time before the Aztec period, but went through six phases of reconstruction and its final form bears the imprint of the Aztec style. The work of excavation was begun in 1925 and lasted three years. It was found that the original nucleus of the pyramid had been covered with several subsequent layers of building. The original structure had been a pyramid in four steps with a height of 25ft and a base between 37ft and 96ft wide. The last rebuilding took place in 1507 under the Aztecs, just a short time before the conquest. Other ancient Mexican peoples also had the custom of renewing their pyramids with a great deal of ceremony every 52 years, the period of the "Mexican Century". Because of this it was possible to count back 52 years four times and arrive at the year 1299 as the year of the first rebuilding. The nucleus of the pyramid must date from between A.D.1200 and 1300, according to this reckoning. It is believed that it was built by the Chichimecs.

As new outer layers were repeatedly built on, the pyramid grew tremendously in size. Today the base measures 192ft by 155ft and it is 63ft high. The main axis, like Teotihuacán, lies at an angle of 17 degrees north of west to point towards the zenith setting of the sun.

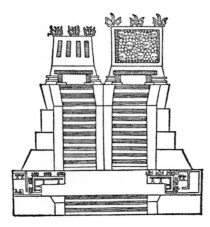

The main temple-pyramid in Tenochtitlán with the temples of Tlaloc and Huitzilopochtli

Aztec symbol for raging war. At the mouth of the skull is the hieroglyph for 'burning water' and higher up on the head is the hieroglyph for 'smoking mirror', one of the names for Tezcatlipoca

On two sides of the pyramid next to stone altars there are two coiled snakes. Their heads gaze towards the point where the sun sinks below the horizon at the winter and summer solstices. The site is thought to have been dedicated to the setting sun in view of the fact that the two menacing "fire serpents", Xiuhcoatl, face in that direction. The Aztecs believed that when the sun sank below the horizon it was swallowed by the earth. During the night it had to do battle with "countless warriors" who were changed into stars. It then appeared new born on the eastern horizon as the victor next morning. There is a stone bank surrounding the pyramid on three sides which has 138 snakes on it. A similar "snake wall", or coatepantli, is supposed to have stood in the main square of Tenochtitlán. We also know that Cortés had the wooden temple on the Pyramid of Tenayuca burned.

About two miles from Tenayuca there is a pyramid standing in the middle of the little village of Santa Cecilia which has been excavated and restored in recent years like the one at Tenayuca. It is much smaller, but it was the only one on the Plateau of Anahuác whose temple could be restored, since it was built in stone. This is how we should picture a temple-pyramid in Aztec times. The harmony of temple and pyramid must have made even a site like Teotihuacán something far more impressive for the early observer than it is for us who can see no more than the bare pyramid base.

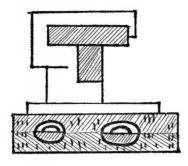

Hieroglyph of the city of Calixtlahuaca. The name means 'houses in the plain', from the words *calli* (house) and *ixtlahuaca* (plain)

5   Calixtlahuaca

The small number of buildings which have survived from Aztec times includes the religious sites of Calixtlahuaca, particularly the round temple-pyramid. There were round buildings in other places in the Aztec period, all of them dedicated to Quetzalcoatl in his identity as the God of Wind. The wind travels across the land in the spiral of a whirlwind, which is a common sight on the Mexican Plateau. The cross-section of a snail-shell, that is a spiral, is for this reason a symbolic decoration of the Wind God.

Calixtlahuaca was founded long before the time of the Aztecs. The site includes three large complexes: human dwellings, a rectangular pyramid and its associated buildings, and the great round pyramid with a ceremonial skull-rack. The site is thought to have been originally the work of the Matlatzincas, a tribe belonging to the great family of the Otomí, although some finds seem to be from the Archaic Period. In any case, the town grew up over several different periods of building. The third shows signs of Toltec influence. After it was conquered by Axayacatl in the year 1476, it was entirely rebuilt in the Aztec style.

The most important building is the four-stepped round pyramid which is 37ft high and 68ft in diameter at ground level. A large platform was built in front

Cross-section of the round pyramid with the temple of Quetzalcoatl as the Wind God in Calixtlahuaca which has been built over several times

of the stairway, which faces east towards the home of the wind. A stone figure of the wind-god in human form was found on it, broken into many pieces but otherwise in good condition. He is wearing a strange mask resembling a duck's beak. The stone skull-rack near the pyramid is laid out in the shape of a cross with walls decorated with skulls. In the middle there is a hollow space to receive the ashes. This skull-rack is a stone symbol for the giant skull-racks of the Aztecs where the heads of sacrificed men were piled up in vast numbers.

Quetzalcoatl as the Wind God (Codex Magliabecchi). Quetzalcoatl appears in a great variety of forms

6 Malinalco

The cliff-temple of Malinalco is a sacred building from the Aztec Period. Like Calixtlahuaca it is in the highlands of Toluca. According to an Aztec chronicle it took fifteen years to build, and was completed a short time before the Spanish conquest. This temple is a unique example of Aztec skill in architecture and stone-masonry. The chambers, stairways and platforms, and even the sculptures of jaguars and eagles which decorate them, have all been carved from the living rock, like the cliff-temples of Egypt or Asia. Apart from one other less important place, the temple of Tetzcotzingo, this is the only example of a cliff-temple in Middle America. It is an incredible achievement when one realises that the Aztecs were still a basically stone-age people, having no metal tools. Up till the present we have been unable to discover for certain to whom this site was dedicated.

The temple is carved out of a cliff-face rising more than 400ft above the little town of Malinalco. Stone jaguars cut from the same rock squat each side of the stairway leading up to it. Inside the almost round cella is a low stone platform with eagle-skins shaped in the rock lying on it. These and the realistically imitated fur on the jaguars suggest that this may have been a centre of an Aztec order of warriors know as the Order of Eagle and Jaguar Warriors. "As a reward for

A knight of the Order of the Eagle in his eagle-type battle dress

A knight of the Order of the Tiger in battle dress
made out of jaguar skin

merit in war and as an encouragement, the Mexicans had three orders the Order
of Princes, the Order of the Eagle, and the Order of the Tiger", Clavigero writes,
"the knights of the Order of the Tiger could be recognised by the uniform they
wore, which looked like a tiger-skin (or a jaguar-skin). However, this was only
worn for warfare."

In Tenochtitlán the "warrior houses" came under the special protection of the
god Tezcatlipoca, with his "smoking mirror", who was also allied to the cave-
god Tepeyolotl or "heart of the mountains". It is possible, though not proven,
that the cave-god was worshipped in the "artificial cave" of Malinalco. The
entrance to the cella is a dragon's mouth carved in relief into the cliff, and
resembles the cave-entrances shown in Aztec pictographic manuscripts.

The monolithic temple of Malinalco is an artistic achievement which combines
elements of architecture and large-scale sculpture.

7 Xochicalco

Between the destruction of Teotihuacán and the beginning of Tollán, that is about the eighth and ninth centuries A.D., one of the oldest known fortresses in Middle America, which was also a religious centre, was built. This is the city of Xochicalco, which formed a cultural bridge between the end of the Classical Period and the early Post-Classical. Already at the beginning of the ninth century Xochicalco must have been an important trading centre as it lay on the trade routes linking the centres of northern and southern culture. It was only developed into a fortress after the theocratic epoch was over. We know little about the people who built this strategic and religious centre. It is, however, probable that they were a Mixtec-speaking group from the south. Xochicalco means in the Nahuatl language "place of the flower-house". This was the name the Aztecs gave it. Although Xochicalco must have had contacts with the theocratic states of the Mexican Plateau there are sharp differences between this metropolis and Teotihuacán. First of all, Xochicalco was the northern-most outpost and bulwark of the southern civilisations. The general lay-out is reminiscent of Monte Albán, a Zapotec site, and the reliefs with their graceful curving lines bear a strong resemblance to the craftsmanship of the Mayas.

Xochicalco lies 430ft above a wide plain on a sugar-loaf mountain among the foothills of the volcano Ajusco, in the state of Morelos 25 miles from Cuerna-vaca. The builders of this mighty and extensive mountain stronghold have used the natural form of the mountain, and as at Monte Albán they have created a new landscape by excavating and piling up the soil. We can clearly distinguish two extensive separate complexes of buildings. The temple pyramid, La Malinche, stands on an artificially flattened space, and from it a road leads along the edge of the mountainside to a large ball-court with several buildings with courtyards and small platforms attached to it. Twenty huge stone pedestals stand on one side of the road joining "La Malinche" and the ball-court.

The first description of Xochicalco dates from the year 1791 by Father José Antonio Alzate y Ramírez. It drew Alexander von Humboldt's attention to the place, and he visited and described it too. Since that time painstaking excava-tions have been made by Mexican archaeologists and many buildings have been restored. Particular trouble was taken with the main temple-pyramid, which measures 69ft along its base on the north and south sides and 61ft on the east and west sides. In its present state it is 54½ft high. However, we must remember that only the lower part of the wall is left of the temple which formerly stood on the platform. The stairway leading to the temple points in the direction of

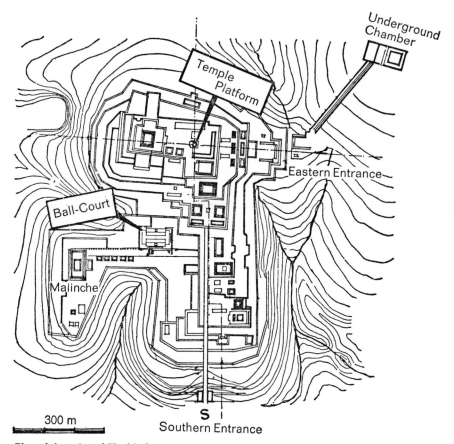

Underground Chamber

Temple Platform

Eastern Entrance

Ball-Court

Malinche

300 m

S
Southern Entrance

Plan of the ruins of Xochicalco

the setting sun. The base of the pyramid is in two parts: the lower half projects outwards, and the upper half is vertical with a sloping cornice at the top. The nine-feet-high lower half is faced with slabs of extraordinarily hard andesite in very varied colours. They have been fitted together without mortar, but the joints are scarely visible. After the building was completed, reliefs 3 or 4 inches deep were carved into these stones in the form of a frieze. They chiefly represent plumed serpents which surround the base with their bodies and have their heads at the pyramid corners. Priests sit cross-legged between the serpents' coils wearing elaborately built-up head-dresses which seem particularly close to Mayan designs. There is also a line of reliefs on the cornice which depict squat-

The Sun Stone, also called the Aztec Calendar-Stone, is 12 feet in diameter. It is a monument to the sun. In the middle is the Sun God surrounded by the symbol '4 movement'. It is called a 'calendar-stone' because of the twenty day-signs in a circle round the sun. Symbols of blood, flowers and precious stones, which are connected with the sun-cult, complete the design

ting warriors with spears and shields alternating with hieroglyphs and symbolic signs.

Among the hieroglyphs, the glyph for "9 rains" occurs several times. The sign for "rain" together with the number 9 also appears repeatedly in Teotihuacán. There the combination of 9 and rain was used to express the name of the rain god, but the Mayan name for the rain god also contained the figure 9.

The most recent excavations in Xochicalco have shown that the culture of the unknown people who lived here must have been closely related to that of the Mayas. This is indicated by the ball-court, where the playing surface slopes upwards towards the outer edges and bears a striking resemblance to the ball-court of Copán in Honduras. Recent work has also shown that Xochicalco must have existed as a religious centre from very early times, but was turned into a defensive stronghold only a short time before the Spanish conquest. Xochicalco is a particularly interesting source of information as the meeting-place of northern and southern cultures.

II Religious Monuments of the Gulf-Coast

La Venta culture 800 B.C. - 400 B.C.
Tajín culture 0 - A.D. 1200

8 La Venta, Tres Zapotes, Cerro de las Mesas

A lowland region with a uniformly hot tropical climate stretches from the middle of the contemporary state of Tamaulipas along the whole coast of the Gulf of Mexico to the states of Veracruz and Tabasco. Important high cultures had already developed in this fertile area in early times. Some of them were still in their fullest flowering at the time when the Spanish reached the Mexican coast. These cultures were very different from the theocratic society of Teotihuacán and the militaristic traditions of the Toltecs and Aztecs.

Three cultures stand out clearly on the Gulf Coast: the culture of the Huastecs, the Tajín culture, and the culture of the Olmecs. They differ from one another in their individual styles of pottery, sculpture, painting and architecture. The most highly regarded are the Olmecs for their so-called "La Venta" culture and the Tajín culture. Monuments have survived in this region which are of outstanding value not just from an archaeological point of view, but perhaps even more as works of art.

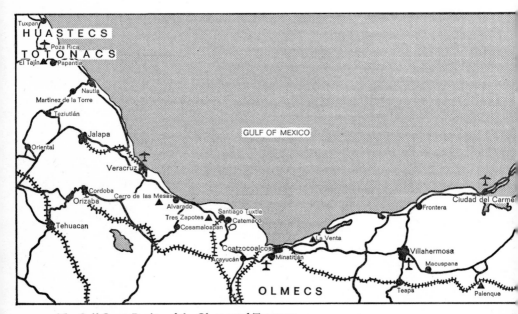

The Gulf Coast. Region of the Olmecs and Totonacs

The culture of the Olmecs, also called the "La Venta" culture after the most important site where finds relating to them have been discovered, remains largely a mystery. It has not been possible to establish for certain who the Olmecs really were. The period of Olmec culture reaches back into Archaic times, and it is widely thought that it may have been a sort of 'mother culture' from which other pre-Columbian cultures gradually developed. Olmec, meaning 'people from the land of rubber', was the name the Aztecs gave these people of the paradisical land on the Gulf Coast. We do not know what they called themselves. A culture developed amazingly early in this fertile though very hot region, and in the time of the Aztecs it had already passed its peak.

Centuries earlier than all the other Indian nations in Middle America, the Olmecs began to create their unique kind of art, and must certainly have stimulated successor cultures to create their own great artistic achievements. This refers mainly to carvings of massive stone monuments. In comparison to these, the Olmecs' architecture seems surprisingly backward, and they cannot be considered great builders at all. Nevertheless, we cannot pass over them and their culture even though this book is chiefly concerned with the great architectural achievements of ancient Mexico.

Radiocarbon dating has shown that La Venta was already developed between 800 and 400 B.C., and perhaps even earlier than this. Fortunately, the discoveries have included objects made of organic materials, which are essential for this method. These particular finds were made on three expeditions organised by the Smithsonian Institution of Washington D.C. and led by M. W. Stirling. In 1938 they went to Tres Zapotes on the bank of the San Juan River in the state of Veracruz, and in 1939 and 1940 to other points 60 miles north-west of Tres Zapotes at Cerro de las Mesas. The most important place, La Venta, which was excavated during the same period, is on an island about 4 miles across in the swampland of the Tonalá River in the state of Tabasco.

The architectural remains to be found at La Venta are interesting. There are square earth-pyramids and round mounds (the main pyramid has proved to be cone-shaped; in fact, it was built like a volcano). In La Venta these mounds are of just plain earth, but the ones at Tres Zapotes have a stone facing, and there are similar structures at the Classical site of Cerro de las Mesas with an outer layer made of a kind of stucco consisting of lime from crushed sea-shells and sand.

As these places, particularly La Venta, are so very inaccessible, it was decided to move the monumental stone sculptures to open-air museums. The ones from La Venta have been set out on a superb site very near Villahermosa, where they stand surrounded by tropical vegetation just as they were discovered. They have been carved from giant blocks of basalt into monumental heads, altars and inscribed stelae. The Olmecs had to move these monolithic sculptures weighing from 20 to as much as 50 tons from the Tuxtla Mountains through 80 miles of jungle, using only the most primitive of means. Even the strange floor-mosaic of a stylised jaguar head has been rebuilt at Villahermosa. However, by far the most powerful and expressive objects there are the monumental stone heads. At Jalapa there is a similar museum for the objects found at Tres Zapotes and Cerro de las Mesas.

The heads are up to 9ft high, and all of them are carved in the same remarkable style. Their noses are flat and they have thick, full lips, deep-set eyes and noses set very low. The smaller carvings of the Olmecs show these mongoloid features in an even more pronounced form. Because of their babyish expression, these faces found on ceremonial axes, masks and small jade figures are called 'baby-faces'. It is surprising that the Olmecs should have used mostly jade, a very hard stone, for their small-scale carvings. The biggest collection of jade objects ever found in Mexico was discovered at Cerro de las Mesas. The 782 figures included some of the largest of this type. There are some with jaguar-like features as well as the babyish look, and many archaeologists think they may well actually represent jaguars. They could be images of a jaguar god or an ancestor in the shape of a jaguar-cub, which is suggested by the fact thet he has not yet grown any teeth. Some of the stone altars of La Venta have low relief carvings of jaguar-mouths too. This ancestor may have been the ancient cave god whom the Aztecs called Tepeyolotl, or 'heart of the mountains'. He had the form of a jaguar and came from the south of Mexico. It is quite possible that he was the same as the cave god to whom offerings were made at Malinalco. The entrance to the inner chamber there passes through a relief representing a wide-open jaguar's mouth.

The mysterious Olmec people emerges from the darkness of the Archaic Period and amazes us from the first with works of art which are outstanding for their power and expressiveness. While one could say that the art of the Maya loses itself in ornamentation and an almost baroque lightness, the art of the Olmecs seems full of virile strength.

Olmec head in the museum-park of Jalapa

27 and 28 Altar and stone Olmec head found in La Venta and now in the
open-air museum of Villahermosa

Torso of an Olmec monumental figure in Jalapa

30 and 31 Torso, probably of a jaguar, and a gigantic stone sculpture of a tortoise from Tres Zapotes, in Jalapa

33 Building with spiral patterns as decoration, El Tajín

34 On the right the great Niche Pyramid, on the left the area called Tajín Chico

35   Terracotta figure of a woman who died in childbirth. Remojadas style from the state
     of Veracruz

36 Terracotta figure of a smiling skeleton. Remo
style, from the state of Veracruz. Remojodas i
name of a site discovered near Veracruz after wh
particular style of pottery has been named

37 An open and a closed stone 'yoke', from the state of Veracruz

9 El Tajín

A civilisation grew up in the middle of what is now the modern state of Vera-cruz which is called the Tajín culture, after its main pyramid and the large area where its ruins are found. It is also called the culture of the Totonacs, but recent research has shown that although El Tajín lies in the region they occupied, they were not its true representatives. These were a separate people about whom very little is known, and the Totonacs only appear in the last phase of develop-ment of the Tajín culture. There are parallels with the culture of Teotihuacán, but there are also many features which suggest Olmec influences. However, because the two areas lie so close together this does not mean very much. Characteristic features of the Olmec style also appear among their other neigh-bours, including the Zapotecs and the Mayas.

The Totonacs, who still inhabit this region, gave the name El Tajín, or 'lightning', to the great temple-pyramid situated about five miles south of Papantla and approximately the same distance from the important oil-produc-ing centre of Poza Rica. It is a region of dense tropical vegetation and large vanilla plantations. The whole archaeological area round the pyramid, covering 136 acres, is now called El Tajín as well, and is one of the largest and most important sites in Mexico. A completely individual architectural and art style developed here and spread widely to other regions. One of its main characteristic features is the niche. This is not only used to decorate the so-called 'Great Tajín', or Niche Pyramid, but also appears on other buildings of the extensive ruined city.

The main centre occupies an area of 40,000 square yards. The site is in a valley which is open to the south, but surrounded by hills on the other three sides. The hills were included in the general lay-out and there are buildings on all of them, but they now lie smothered by dense tropical vegetation which has not yet been cleared.

The 'Great Tajín' is a seven-layer pyramid with a base 120ft square and measuring 60ft in height including the temple, which is still discernible. The vertical walls of each layer are faced with slabs of sedimentary rock, and are decorated with square niches. The steeply-rising stairway was added later, and is raised well above the terraces so that it leads directly to the temple in a single flight decorated with several niches. The idea that formerly there were figures standing in the niches has proved to be wrong. The niche is a purely ornamental element characteristic of the Tajín style in buildings. There are 364 of them, not counting those on the stairway. This number is thought to be connected with the Mexican calendar, which the Tajín culture probably took from the Olmecs. The Maya and the Zapotecs also used niches as decoration, but the builders of the 'Great Tajín' made the niche an architectural leitmotiv which is employed on all seven steps of the great pyramid.

Close to the Niche Pyramid is the so-called Tajín Chico, a later group of buildings that includes the Pillar Building. It is perhaps the most magnificent group of the entire city. The complex is divided into three sections. The Pillar Building itself consists of a hall of pillars and a few minor buildings which occupy a platform on a mound. The West Court, an area of 13,200 square yards, is flanked on the north, south and west sides by wide platforms and buildings which have not yet been excavated. The third complex includes the 'Tunnel House', a building resembling a temple from whose west side two tunnels lead up to the temple on the pyramid. All the buildings were faced with stone slabs and blocks of sandstone and basalt. One of them is 36ft long. The materials had to be brought from the banks of the Rio Cazones, a distance of 22 miles as the crow flies.

Many buildings in the city are decorated with fret patterns. Even the niches and balustrades on either side of the stairway on the 'Great Tajín' have this decoration. All of them originally had a covering of yellow, red, black or blue stucco. The low reliefs, which show an extraordinary degree of skill, were also brightly coloured. These are found in the ball-court and the Niche Pyramid, but those on the pillars in the Pillar Building are the most magnificently com-

The heart-sacrifice. The priest cuts the victim's heart out with an obsidian knife

Sacrifice by throwing spears. The sacrificial priest is wearing a mask representing the god of death and is carrying a shield and two spears

posed. They show gods with masks, skeletons and realistic scenes from daily life including people in splendid clothes, sacrifices, and the method of flattening the skull of a child. This was a custom which also existed among the Maya.

The Tajín culture had its own technique of roof-building using a kind of concrete instead of the perishable materials employed for most of the temples of other high cultures. It consisted of lime from crushed sea-shells, finely ground pumice-stone, sand, straw, and small pieces of wood. The slabs were cast in wooden moulds and made between 2 and 4 inches thick. Three or four of these were laid on top of one another to make a roof. The rooms which were covered with these could not be bigger than 90 square yards or more than 16ft wide.

The climate here is exceptionally wet and excavations can only be carried out during the dry season, which means that progress is slow and the cost of operations very high. Surprisingly enough, no human bones or burial-places have been discovered yet. On the other hand there have been a number of interesting finds such as the many artistically decorated votive axes made from the hardest stone, richly carved stone yokes, and the extremely finely worked 'palmas', so named because they are shaped like palm-leaves. Recent research has shown that axes, yokes and 'palmas' were used in connection with a ritual ball game played by many Mexican peoples.

This important religious centre survived the great upheaval that struck many cities at the end of the Classic Period and its influence continued to be felt in other major Mesoamerican centres.

III Religious Monuments of the South

Zapotec culture 400 B.C. - A.D. 800
Mixtec culture A. D. 800 - 1521
Maya culture 1000 B.C. - A.D. 1546

The state of Oaxaca. Region of the Zapotecs and Mixtecs

10   Monte Albán

The culture of the Zapotecs, which developed in the south of Mexico around the Valley of Oaxaca, in the state of Oaxaca, is also counted among the theocratic civilisations of Mexico.

The enormous archaeological region which this people left behind them extends over every part of the state of Oaxaca, but is particularly important on the broad plateau reaching an average altitude of 5000ft on which the town of Oaxaca stands. So far it has been possible to study only a few of the 200 ruined sites known to archaeologists. These include Etla, Xoxo, Yagul and above all Monte Albán and Mitla. The centre of the entire archaeological area and the most important religious monument of the Zapotecs is Monte Albán.

Continual progress in the excavations at Monte Albán has proved that there was contact between the Zapotecs and both the Olmecs and the early Maya. However, in spite of finds going back to the earliest times, the history of the Zapotecs remains a mystery to us. We can only assume that there was more than one people involved, and that the Zapotecs replaced the creators of the first and second cultural periods, whose name we do not know, or that they were later absorbed by the Zapotecs. Since there are strong variations in style according to the age of objects discovered here, this culture, known gene-

Hieroglyphs on the building at Monte Albán which stands on its own with a different form and orientation from the others. The style is Period II. The middle part of the glyph means a mountain. Above it is a glyph which probably means the place, and underneath an upsidedown head

rally as the 'Zapotec Culture', is divided into periods as is the Teotihuacán culture. However, it can be demonstrated beyond doubt that only the third and fourth periods, occuring between the fourth and fifteenth centuries A.D. are in fact Zapotec. The first and second periods extend from the sixth century B.C. to the fourth century A.D. The fifth and last period is ascribed to the Mixtecs.

Even though this division is not accepted unconditionally by every authority in the field, they are all agreed that the Zapotecs were a nation of superb architects. Their major achievement lay not in the particular design of individual buildings, but in the grandeur of conception with which Monte Albán was laid out, depending as it does on a fine feeling for spatial relationships. The design of this vast and architecturally daring religious site must have been planned – from the laying of the first stone up to its completion – according to one single concept which maintains a harmony between the many similarly shaped buildings.

To this day there are still approximately 120,000 Indians living in the state of Oaxaca who speak the Zapotec language – descendants of the builders of the greatest sacred place of the Zapotecs. They are among the most intelligent people of Mexico. The superior character and intellectual capacity of these people was already noticed by the Spaniards when setting up a stronghold in Oaxaca, shortly after the conquest of Mexico. Brightly-patterned Zapotec

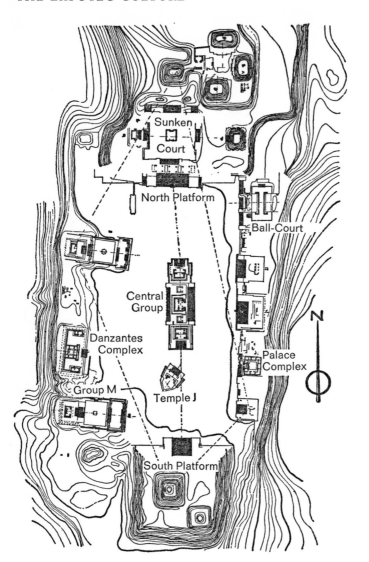

Plan of the ruins of
Monte Albán

woven textiles and black clay figures and pots are still produced with the refined
skill of the ancient Indians as they were hundreds of years ago, and are greatly
prized throughout Mexico.

The central temple-site of Monte Albán is situated on an artificially flattened
mountain about 1200ft above the valley of Oaxaca. The other sites extend over

an area of 15 square miles and include a number of other artificial platforms, palaces, burial chambers and many fortifications. Under the leadership of the Mexican Alfonso Caso archaeologists have been working for a period of more than thirty-five years on uncovering and restoring the central site. Alfonso Caso, who has devoted his life to the study of Monte Albán, made a discovery in 1932 which caused as great a sensation in the world of Mexican antiquities as the uncovering of Tutankhamen's tomb in Egypt: it was Tomb No. 7, a structure which was built by the Zapotecs but later used by the Mixtecs as a mausoleum for their highest dignitaries. More than five hundred objects were found there, including the largest gold treasure ever discovered in Mexico.

At the middle point of the sacred area on Monte Albán stands the so-called 'Acropolis', a central group of buildings. The main temple, however, is not here but on the North Platform, a space 50,000 square yards in an area which adjoins a sunken courtyard further to the north. Somewhat to one side of the long axis, which determines the arrangement of all the other buildings, there is a peculiar building standing at 45 degrees to the rest, known as the Observatory. The ball-court lying on the eastern side of the vast truncated mountain has upward-sloping terraces without stone rings. It is strongly reminiscent of classic Mayan ball-courts, for example, the one at Copán in Honduras.

The grandiose architecture of Monte Albán is particularly distinguished by a system of unusually broad flights of steps. The steps leading to the large main temple are 45 yards wide; this is the widest ancient stairway in Central America. This massively constructed flight of steps in front of the building counterbalances the gigantic round pillars of the main temple. They have a diameter of 6ft, but only the stumps are left now.

The axes of all the buildings on Monte Albán run parallel to one another. The levels of the various groups interrelate to show the nature of the whole complex and give it its particular quality. The buildings at the middle of the site are lower than those at the edges.

The outstanding architectural and artistic features of Monte Albán include the carved stone covering of an earth pyramid on the west side of the great open square. This structure had a facing of stone slabs bearing reliefs. A few of these were still found in place, and others were discovered in piles of rubble scattered around. There are low reliefs carved on these slabs, life-size figures with faces indicating Olmec influence. They are portrayed in extraordinarily grotesque positions, and are known for this reason as *Danzantes*, i.e. dancers. A few slabs and stelae are also decorated with hieroglyphs which are different from those of the Maya and Aztecs, and are not understood. Only the numbers can be read and they are expressed in dots and dashes like those of the Aztecs. Every dot signifies one unit, every dash five, and zero is represented by a shell. The hieroglyphs on the monuments of Monte Albán are considered by Alfonso Caso to be considerably older than the earliest surviving Mayan hieroglyphs. One can therefore feel reasonably sure that the *Danzantes* belong to the early period of Monte Albán.

The chief deity of the Zapotecs, the Rain God Cocijo, represents another Olmec feature of the earlier periods of Monte Albán. He was a mythical being, a jaguar god, a 'man-eating beast' reminding one of the 'jaguar god in human form' of La Venta. Contact with Mayan culture is suggested by single free-standing stelae which still bear undecipherable hieroglyphs, possibly commemorating historical events.

Together with the extraordinarily numerous and imposing structures above ground, there is also a great number of underground shrines built in a 'T' or cross-shape, and many burial chambers; for this reason Monte Albán was also known as a 'settlement of cave-dwellers'. These remains date from a later period. They belong to the fourth period, during which Monte Albán began to decline. Finally the Zapotecs were driven out by the Mixtecs. In the succeeding period the Mixtecs developed the art of building underground to a high level, and were the only civilised people in Mesoamerica to do so.

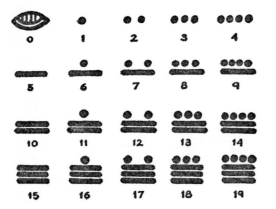

Mayan system of writing numbers from 0–19. The Mayas used dots and dashes in exactly the same way as the Aztecs. They were for ordinary practical purposes, while priests and learned men drew human heads. With the dot and dash system 20 symbols were needed, but with the heads only the 14 symbols from 0 to 13 were necessary because to count further jaw-bones were added to the heads from 4 to 9. These were the head-symbols for 14 to 19

11 Mitla

We know as little about the history of the Mixtecs as we do about the Zapotecs. It is certain that they go back to very early times. The mythical homeland of the Mixtecs is supposed to have been 'Cloudland' or Mictlan, the 'Place of the Dead'. They gradually advanced into the mountainous neighbouring territory and eventually mixed with the Zapotecs.

There were Mixtec communities on the central highlands of Mexico as early as the Toltec period who, particularly in the state of Puebla and above all in Cholula had a tradition of craftsmanship. Such superb examples of Mixtec goldsmithing, mosaics and ceramics have survived that it is customary today to talk of a Mixtec-Puebla culture. Similarly, their pictographic manuscripts, which are readily distinguishable from those of the Maya, show great mastery. Two particularly colourful Mixtec manuscripts, the 'Codex Vindobonensis' and the 'Codex Becker I' are kept in Vienna. They concern themes from mythology and ancient history, and are exceedingly complex. The colours have been made more intense by applying a thin white coat of plaster wash to the material (made from the lining of mulberry-bark) before painting on it.

Many scholars set the date of earliest occupation of the Mixtecs of Monte Albán in A.D. 1000; others believe that it did not begin until the 14th century. By this time development in the thousand-year-old art of the Zapotecs had already come to an end. Even the buildings, tombs and underground religious sanctuaries which were designed by Zapotecs bear new forms suggesting occupation by the Mixtecs. This applies also to the famous Tomb No. 7 mentioned earlier. It was built by the Zapotecs but the precious objects found there were of Mixtec origin.

When the Mixtecs advanced into the broad valley of Oaxaca, they came everywhere upon temples and palaces. Even the town of Mitla, 25 miles from Oaxaca, was already in existence and known to the Zapotecs as Lyobaa. The Mixtecs renamed it Mitla, presumably in memory of Mictlan, the 'Place of the Dead'.

Mitla really is a city of the dead, containing a huge number of graves. Five groups of buildings stand out among the many remains of houses. The groups stand in two pairs close together with the fifth separated from the others by the small Río de Mitla. There is a church built within the walls of one of the temples by the Spanish of the colonial period, with the mud huts of the Indian villagers standing round it. The most important building in Mitla is the 'Palace of Pillars', known as the 'Erechtheion of America'. This building, and the others from the

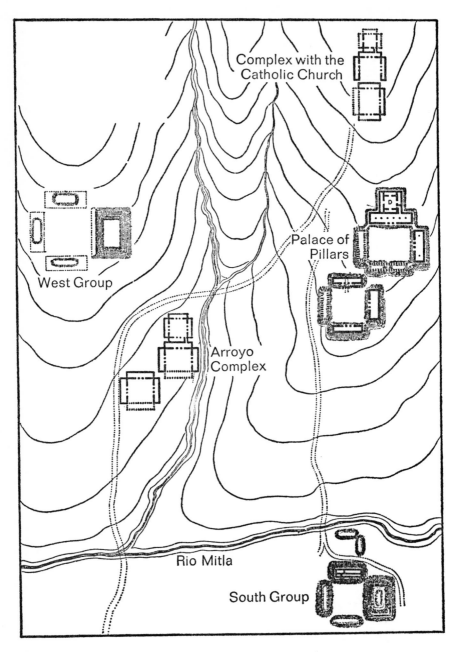

Plan of the ruins of Mitla

central groups too, have been known for a long time. The first description, by Burgoa, dates from 1644. There are other, later descriptions by Alexander von Humboldt, Charnay, Seler and Holmes.

In the time of the Zapotecs Mitla was already a city of the dead where kings and priests were interred in vaults. The Palace of Pillars was the holy of holies of this city, a mysterious structure intended only for the high priest, 'the great seer' Uijatáo, whom Eduard Seler called: 'The living image of the godhead or its deputy.' He lived here in the greatest seclusion, never showing himself to the people.

A broad steep flight of steps leads directly to the great Hall of Pillars over a substructure which is almost as high as the rooms of the palace, a height of about five feet. The walls are of pale grey trachyte, as in the other rooms. There are no windows, but the walls are decorated with a profusion of mosaics. There is abstract ornamentation on the façade rather like that of Maya towns in Yucatán, but the main decoration is reserved for the inner walls. Three strips set into them one above the other bearing what appears to be a mosaic design of meandering steps, occupy the upper half of the walls all the way round the room. The patterns are remarkably varied; fourteen motifs have been counted. In fact these mosaic patterns do not consist of many small stones set together. The pattern has been carved with such precision on carefully fitted-together stone slabs that it has the appearance of countless mosaic tesserae fixed to a base. The background colour of these 'mosaic strips', as one might be permitted to call them, was dark red, while the splendid patterns were yellow, brown and white in colour.

All these areas of mosaic are not just ornamentation pure and simple, but represent an important element in a very rigorous architectural style. The walls do not appear at all monotonous; on the contrary, the rich decoration is full of life and gives them something of the effect of a Persian carpet. This peculiar technique is quite unique. It was brought to the highest level of precision not only in the Palace of Pillars but also in other buildings intended for the priests or the king when he made a visit to Mitla. Even in the Mixtec period, however, his residence remained at Monte Albán.

Strangely enough the walls of the Hall of Pillars in the Palace of Pillars are undecorated. There is certainly a definite intention behind the design of this room. Its round pillars become slightly conical towards the top and have the effect of directing the eye upwards. To stress the horizontal element with strips of ornamentation would only have disturbed the overall effect. In this way the plainness of this room counterbalances the others; it becomes a peaceful pole to the other profusely decorated chambers.

We might perhaps be surprised that the Zapotecs and Mixtecs should have devoted so much care to the construction of a city of the dead. But even Diodorus Siculus has said: 'There are nations which erect splendid palaces for their dead. Since life on earth is so short and impermanent, they say, it is not worth the trouble to build in such a style for the living.'

The Maya

In order to form a clearer idea of the differences between the various ancient Mexican cultures and the stages of their development, it is possible to make comparisons between the high cultures of the Old and New Worlds. One could say that the artistically gifted Toltecs were like the Etruscans, and the war-like Aztecs, who developed their political power as successors to the Toltecs, were like the Romans. The Maya, with their great intellectual gifts, could justly be called the 'Greeks of America' for the powerful influence they had on the whole culture of Middle America. Naturally, these comparisons only hold in a very general way. There was absolutely no similarity in the details of development in America and the Mediterranean countries nor in the time-scale. The people and environments on each side of the ocean were fundamentally different, but there are certain invariable natural laws governing the growth of cultures. People anywhere in the world who have reached the same stage of their development are linked by invisible bonds which guide them inevitably towards the same destiny.

We should also picture the 'empire' of the Maya as something very similar to the Greek city-state, or polis. At one time it was usual to talk about an 'Old Empire' and a 'New Empire' of the Maya, but these terms have now completely gone out of use. There never was an 'empire' of the Maya in our sense of the word. The individual city-states never made up a real political unit, but had a sort of federal status based on the common culture which they all shared, while each province was independent.

These city-states always centred round the temple-pyramids and buildings closely involved with the religious sphere, such as palaces for priests and kings and the houses of artisans and learned men. The ordinary people were peasants living in modest settlements scattered across the area where they had their fields. The peasants had no civil rights and no voice in questions of government, unlike the peasants of Greece.

But who were the Maya? Where did they come from? Their ancestors must have come like the ancestors of all the Indians of America from Asia, long before they had learned the art of agriculture and began to evolve their later high civilisation. At the time of the beginning of the Christian Era there were Indian tribes living on the plateau of Guatemala, in Honduras, El Salvador and south-

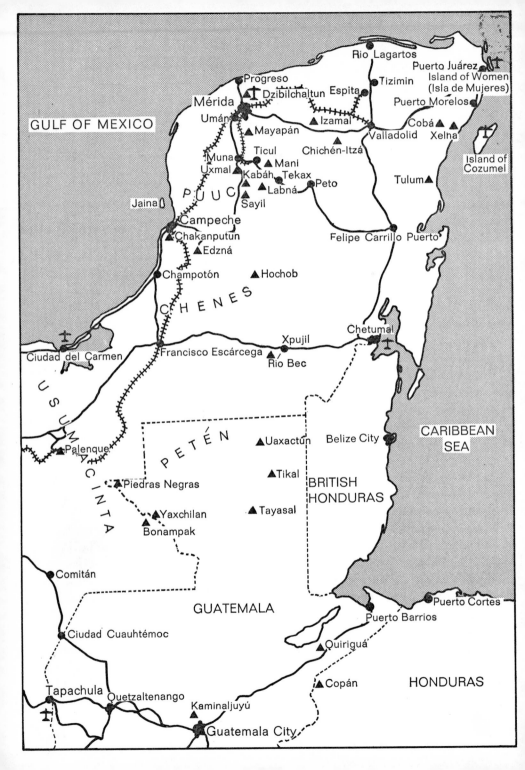

ern Mexico whose languages had a common root in the Mayan language, which was spoken in many different dialects as it still is today. About twenty Indian tribes in this area speak dialects which belong to the great Mayan phylum. Even the Huastecs, who live near Tampico in Veracruz, a long way from the Maya heartland, speak a Mayan tongue. Often there are such strong differences between dialects that the various tribes find it difficult to understand one another. However, it appears from the hieroglyphs on buildings and stelae that the written language used by educated people, in other words the priests and learned men, was the same in all the various Maya cities.

But the question still remains whether the Maya, who created the great monuments in the jungle of Chiapas and Tabasco, at Petén in Guatemala, in the jungles of Honduras and later in the rocky bush-country of Yucatán, came from the Plateau of Guatemala or whether they branched off from the mysterious Olmecs and settled these regions from the Gulf Coast. If this is what happened it must have been very early on, because a high culture like that of the Maya, which reached its fullest development between A.D. 300 and 900, could hardly, in the middle of the jungle, spring from nothing.

Just as Hellas was able to get ideas and inspiration from the Phoenicians, Cretans and Egyptians, the Maya were also stimulated to ever greater achievements by contact with other peoples, especially in the later period. When examples of Mexican craftsmanship reached the Maya they did not just slavishly copy them, but used the ideas to develop entirely new and original forms. Everything which the Mayans did in the way of art, writing or architecture was even more closely bound up with the calendar than was the case with any of the other nations of the Mexican Plateau.

The Maya are generally considered the inventors of the Mexican calendar, but many people now believe that the Olmecs already had a calendar, and this was taken over by the Maya and then developed to its later high level of accuracy. All agrarian cultures are extremely interested in following the seasons of the year. In the tropics it is essential to know when the rainy season begins because the times for sowing and harvesting depend on it. The only reliable way of knowing when it is due is by astronomical observations. We know that the Maya made such observations from the tower-shaped observatories at Palenque, Uaxactún, Mayapán and Chichén-Itzá. Their tremendous desire to understand the connections between cosmic events is very understandable when one realises how very much they were at the mercy of natural forces living in a tropical area. They believed that human destiny was controlled by cosmic powers, and for this reason the calendar became an important part of their

The gods carry the burden of the years. This is shown in the Mayan hieroglyphs. The picture shows the Mayan god of the number nine

religion. It was revered as a sacred thing, and was also a symbol of the universe. The days were represented on the Mayan calendar by symbols, and each symbol, and therefore each day, was dedicated to a god. The symbols of gods were connected with numbers, which then together made the concept of time. Time was a burden which the gods had to bear. The Mayan view made even gods subordinate to the laws of the Cosmos.

The calendar was a holy book which distinguished between good and evil days, and it supplied a prognostication for every single day. Priests and astrologers could read the destinies of men in it. No course of action was ever undertaken without first consulting the Calendar of Prophecy. Absolutely everything became dependent on the sacred calendar. Work was only started on the construction of temples and other buildings when the calendar indicated that there was no danger of interference from cosmic forces, and it was the task of the artist to keep hostile forces at bay.

Some of the basic features of the Maya calendar can be described here. It depends on three systems or calculations: the *haab* or sun-year with 365 days, the *tzolkin* or 'counting of days' with 260 days, and the Venus-year, calculated by the Mayans to be 584 days, which had the other two systems built into it. Modern measurements estimate the cycle of the Venus-year to take 583 and 92 hundredths days, so we can see how incredibly accurate the Maya were in their calculations.

They used a vigesimal system. The *haab* or sun-year was divided into 18 months of 20 days and five additional unlucky days, or 'days without names'. The *tzolkin* consisted of 13 months of 20 days. The combination of the *haab* and the *tzolkin* gave the exact date. After 52 years or 18,980 days the cycle reaches the same point again and a day has the same name and number in *tzolkin* and *haab*. The number 20 was the basic unit of counting. Twenty years of 360

Schematic representation of the two calendar systems according to Morley. The smaller wheel shows the division of the 260-day year. The 20 day-glyphs are on the outer ring and the 13 day-numbers inside. The right-hand wheel, of which only a segment is shown, represents the 365-day year divided into 18 months of 20 days each and an additional five unlucky days. In the middle are the glyphs of the months

days made a *katún*. Periods of time equivalent to our centuries and millennia were obtained by further multiplying by twenty. The system goes up to 1 *alautún* or 23 milliards and 40 million days. S. G. Morley called the Mayan calendar and their system of numbers, which used the zero a thousand years before the Arabs, "one of the most brilliant creations of the human intellect up to present times".

The latest excavations of Dzibilchaltún in Yucatán have produced a huge number of finds which make the theory of an Old and New Empire of the Maya less and less convincing. It is now known that the beginnings of the culture of the southern provinces, in about A.D. 300, date from the same period as the culture of the northern provinces. A stele just recently discovered in Yucatán bears the date equivalent to A. D. 415, while a continuous series of calendar-dates has survived on temples, stairways and stelae in the southern provinces. The culture of each of these large regions developed independently, though each influenced and stimulated the other, but they reached their peaks at different periods. The cities in Yucatán did not reach their highest level of architectural skill until the splendour of the cities in Petén and the valley of the Usumacinta river was already in decay.

In the southern areas architectural styles show significant variations from city to city. Henri Stierlin points out that it is precisely in these regions that the Maya language is separated into different dialects, and the linguistic frontiers between the Chontalic, Mopanic, Tschortic and Tzeltalic dialects corres pond almost exactly with the lines separating the areas where the various architectural styles appear. In the North, that is, Yucatán, there is only one dialect spoken and the architecture is more unified in style, though variations do still exist. These are grouped under the headings Puuc style, Río Bec style, and Chenes style.

Between the 10th and 12th centuries Yucatán went through a real renaissance after Toltec warriors had invaded the area and introduced Toltec styles into the Mayan tradition. They also introduced a new god into the Mayan pantheon: Quetzalcoatl, or Kukulkán as he was called in Yucatán. His rituals required human sacrifices, and it appears that this was the time when the Maya first began to use hearts as offerings to the gods in larger numbers. Earlier there had only been human sacrifices to the rain-god Tlaloc at particular times, when the victims were drowned in the sacred well or cenote of Chichén-Itzá.

The Maya possessed the finest culture of pre-Hispanic Middle America. It is astonishing that such a comparatively small nation divided into even smaller separate communities could reach such a high level of development in a few centuries, particularly as they were cut off from other peoples and had to make all their discoveries unaided.

Mayan studies are progressing all the time, but are still a long way from reaching any final conclusion. Famous scholars still hold completely opposing views and many problems have still to be solved. Nevertheless, no-one can deny that in their architecture the Maya have left behind examples of their abilities which are beyond all criticism. These buildings have retained their pure artistic glory up to the present day.

Stone slab with a relief of a *danzante*, Monte Albán

39 Temple-pyramid with the stone slabs bearing *danzantes*. Period I of Monte Albán

40 The artificially truncated hill with the temple-sites, Monte Albán

tele from Period I of Monte Albán with glyphs which are not understood. The numbers written with dots and dashes are the same as those of the Aztecs and Maya

42 Stone relief of a figure with Olmec features over a burial-chamber

43 Even the *danzantes* of Monte Albán show Olmec influence

44 Stone lintel above the entrance to a burial-chamber with symbolic signs

45 Entrance to a burial-chamber. It was closed with the stone slab on the left. Monte Albán

46 A small temple, restored, and behind it a pyramid which has not yet been excavated. Monte Albán

47 Underground burial–place in the shape of a cross, Mitla

Room with 'stone-mosaics' in the Palace of the Pillars at Mitla

49 The 'mosaics' in the palace at Mitla are really stone slabs with the patterns cut into them

50 The Hall of Pillars in the Palace of the Pillars has no 'mosaic' decoration

51 The Spanish built a Christian church right inside the walls of Mitla

52 Even the outer walls of the palace and some of the other buildings in Mitla have 'mosaic' decorations

The Great Palace with the observatory tower. Palenque

The Temple of the Foliated Cross at Palenque right on the edge of the jungle

On the right is the Temple of the Cross and on the left is the Sun Temple with a pierced comb on its curved roof. Palenque

56　Detail from the stone low relief along the stairway in an inner court of the palace. Palenque

and 58   Priest with kneeling slaves after a drawing by Catherwood and the same stucco relief today

Catherwood's drawing of the stairway with stone reliefs (below) and stucco reliefs (above). Palenque

60 Stucco head from the burial-chamber of the 'Temple of Inscriptions', Palenque, which was probab
sacrificial offering

Masks of the rain-god as decoration on the façade of the temple of Xlampak

62 The west side of the Great Palace of Sayil in the Puuc style

63 Detail of an ante-chamber with a balustrade frieze

The stylised mask of the rain-god above one of the entrances to the palace of Sayil

65   The walls of these Mayan buildings are sometimes built of piled-up earth with a facing inside and out
stone slabs and pillars. The ornamentation on this corner represents an open serpent's mouth with a hu
head projecting out of it

66 and 67 The triple bulges on the decorative pillars are imitations of the rope bindings of earlier wooden architecture

68 The triumphal arch of Labná is also built in the Puuc style. It marked the place where two parts of the city joined (see also the picture on the cover)

69 On the left is the Temple of Statues with the triumphal arch of Labná on the right

The pyramid has been cleared but not yet restored. The Temple of Statues has a roof comb which is not in the middle but stands above the main façade

71   The Triumphal Arch of Kabáh stands at the end of the ancient Mayan road from Uxmal

The Codz-Pop or Palace of Masks in Kabáh with the trunk-like stone noses of the masks of the rain-god Chac

73 Stylised masks of the rain-god cover the entire front wall of the Palace of Masks in the manner Chenes style

74 The Governor's Palace in Uxmal. The mosaic strip consists of about 20,000 stones

75 Phallic monument and a double-headed jaguar on an altar in front of the Governor's Palace

The Soothsayer Pyramid in Uxmal. The opening into the built-
over temple was made in recent
times

View into the Nunnery Quadrangle

Soothsayer Pyramid seen from
the Nunnery Quadrangle, Uxmal

80 and 81
North building and lower gallery of the n
building of the Nunnery Quadrangle with s
columns

◁ 79   Left the partly-restored Nunnery Quadrangle right the Soothsayer Pyramid

82   Chac masks used as decorative motif on the corners of the buildings of the Nunnery Quadr

83 Carving of a guardian on the west building of the Nunnery Quadrangle. An unusually fine examp
sculpture in the Puuc style among the Maya

84 and 85 Ornament with serpents' heads on a reticulated background which is intended to give the impression of a transparent grille

The pyramid of Kukulkán, known as the Castillo, seen from the Warrior Temple. Chichén-Itzá

Standard-bearer above the head of a plumed serpent on the stairway leading to the Warrior Temple

Warrior Temple with its ante-chamber. It shows a marked resemblance to the temples built by the Toltecs in Tula

90 Free-standing sculpture of a tiger (jaguar) in the vestibule of the lower part of the temple. Jaguar Temple, Chichén-Itzá

91 Platform of the Tigers and Eagles in the foreground, Jaguar Temple in the background

◁ 89 Truncated pyramid structure of the Jaguar Temple in Chichén-Itzá

92 Relief picture of a ball-game on the back wall of the Jaguar Temple, which is also one of the boundary-walls of the ball-court

93 The great ball-court of Chichén-Itzá with a stone ring and a small temple on the narrower side

94 and 95   Stone skulls on the tzompantli, or place where the skulls were placed.

The sacred pool or *cenote* of Chichén-Itzá, a sink-hole formed in the limestone surface of the ground. Human sacrifices were performed here

The Tomb of the Great Priest in the southern part of Chichén-Itzá

nd 99

observatory, known as the Cara-
a cylindrical structure standing on
ries of terraces. On the top there
chamber with 'sighting holes'
ch are set out for astronomical ob-
ations

Buildings belonging to the Nunnery

Doorway with a false arch. Behind it is the observatory

Nunnery of Chichén-Itzá with ornamentation in the Chenes style reaching down to the ground

103   View of the observatory of Chichén-Itzá. It is called Caracol or 'snail' because of the spiral staircase in

12 Palenque

Right in the heart of Middle America lies the Maya country, extending over an area of 125,000 square miles. It covers the whole of Guatemala apart from its west coast, British Honduras or Belize, a part of Honduras and the Mexican states of Campeche, Tabasco, Yucatán, Quintana Roo and part of Chiapas. Palenque is in Chiapas.

Lost in the dense tropical jungle, Palenque was rediscovered by people from the outside world hardly 150 years ago. Nowadays the ruined city is only 5 miles from the railway between Coatzacoalcos and Campeche which was built a few years back, but the tropical forest with trees 100ft high still makes a mighty backdrop to this astonishing scene. The first impression which hits us when we stand in front of the temple-city is hardly less than that which John L. Stephens, the American amateur archaeologist and diplomat describes.

"Among the destruction and decay we could see back into the past", writes Stephens, "see the gloomy forest lighten and imagine every building in its perfection, with its terraces and pyramids, its ornaments carved in stone and painted, magnificent, sublime and awesome, looking out over a never-ending plain. We summoned the strange foreign people sadly looking down at us from the wall back to life. We pictured them in fantastic clothes decked out with feathers as they went up the palace terraces ... Nothing in the story of world history has ever made such a powerful impression on me as the sight of this once great and charming city many miles in circumference, now a forgotten shambles discovered by accident and completely overgrown by trees. It did not even have a name by which you could call it."

The true name of this city has been lost, like those of most Maya cities. Palenque is a Spanish name meaning "palisade village".

Stephens visited Palenque with the the painter Catherwood in 1840, and later published a book with brilliant illustrations by Catherwood called "Incidents of Travel in Central America, Chiapas and Yucatán" which caused a considerable stir. Another American writer had already claimed in a much-read book called "The History of America" that the New World did not possess a single monument or even the remains of a building from before the time of the Conquista, although Alexander von Humboldt in the accounts of his travels in Mexico in 1803 and 1804 had already drawn the attention of learned circles to the vanished cultures of ancient America. Yet even Humboldt had no idea of the existence of the magnificent Maya cities.

Picture of a kneeling Mayan on a stone plaque in Palenque. In his right hand he is holding a stick with a piece of material attached to it and in his left an unknown object

When the Danish archaeologist Frans Blom visited Palenque in 1923, he found the same amazing scene as Stephens: "I wandered from one building to another. They are empty and abandoned now, but were once occupied by great rulers, venerable priests and bustling workers. Water drips from the roofs and clouds of bats sweep by as my echoing footsteps disturb them. Stairways and dark passages lead to underground galleries . . . The first visit to Palenque makes an incredible impression. When you have lived here a while the ruined city becomes a kind of obsession."

Since that time much has been excavated and uncovered, but all round there are still densely overgrown mounds of crumbling pyramids with the ruins of many buildings. Streams flow through the hilly landscape, in some places over stone-built aqueducts or along canals. A lot of the masonry has collapsed, but water still flows through the ancient Mayan channels. Unfortunately the ruins were not treated correctly when they were first discovered. In order to get at the collapsing buildings more easily, the forest was set on fire. In many cases this damaged them even more because the fire dried out the stucco and weakened the mortar between the stones, so that priceless stucco reliefs crumbled and fell away into dust.

In the wet climate of the Maya country it is not enough just to excavate and reconstruct the buildings. They have to be carefully preserved or they may fall into decay again. The tropical forest grows so fast that it will quickly reclaim them unless they are constantly tended. If there is not enough money and labour available to keep the ruins free of the constantly encroaching vegetation, then the work of excavating them will all go for nothing.

Up to now the two main groups of buildings separated by a small stream called the Otolum have been excavated and largely restored. In some places the stream flows underground through a stone-built culvert. This was covered in by means of the 'false' arch which was also used for the chambers of palaces and temples. The Maya had not invented the transferred thrust or 'true' arch.

Unlike the people of the Mexican Plateau, where the temples on top of pyramids were normally built of wood, the Maya developed the technique of constructing temples in stone, and in the fourth century A.D. they made a great step forward by inventing the stone arch. As we have seen, the people of Tajín built flat roofs using a kind of concrete. The Maya adopted a different approach, taking the inside of the straw-thatched huts which Indians in Maya country still build as a starting point. They tried as far as they could to imitate in stone the manner in which wooden beams were used to support the pointed roofs of these huts. The inside of a Mayan arch is therefore a direct imitation of

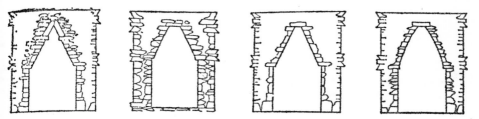

The Mayan arch, or so-called 'false arch', which could be used for the construction of roofs over long rooms but not broad ones

the roof of a *choza*, as the Indian huts are called. In the resulting technique the stones are laid so that the walls slope inwards towards one another until a single stone can be laid across the gap and join them. It is somewhat reminiscent of the megalithic buildings of early Greece, but this is deceptive as the stones would not be enough to support the arch on their own. It is actually the walls, which become more massive towards the top and have a kind of concrete filling, that give the arch its strength. This technique cannot be used to span wide spaces, but the roofs can be made as long as required.

Palenque in particular has very fine examples of these arches. In spite of the rather bulky structure weighing down on a comparatively small enclosed space, buildings constructed in this way seem very light and delicate. This can be seen in the Sun Temple, where there is also a superstructure built in the form of a roof comb which contributes to this effect. Some rooms in the temples and palaces have T-shaped windows, a most unusual feature in Mesoamerican architecture. The doors again show a certain similarity with *chozas*. Often there are two rooms with parallel arches under one massive roof, as for example in the Temple of the Cross. A pierced stone comb rises above the curved roof and gives the building its particular elegance.

Six main temples have been found in Palenque so far. The most important of these are the Temple of the Cross, the Sun Temple, the Temple of the Foliated Cross and the Temple of Inscriptions. These temples are not laid out with reference to any particular point of the compass, nor do they stand along any great avenue like the temple-pyramids flanking the Way of the Dead at Teoti-

Sketch of the pyramid and Temple of Inscriptions in Palenque showing the burial-chamber discovered by Alberto Ruz in 1952

huacán. The lay-out is much more informal. As the Maya had no draught animals and no vehicles, they did not need any roads. Because of this a real garden-city grew up in this hilly landscape among gardens and streams. The palaces and temples lie scattered about at carefully-judged distances from one another in a most effective arrangement.

The most prominent site was reserved for the Main Palace. Standing on an artificially-raised platform close to the middle of the city, it dominates the entire scene. The pyramids and temples are grouped round it, while in the background stands the great green wall of the jungle. The palace itself is dominated by a four-storeyed square tower, which is the observatory. In one of the inner courts two sandstone stelae with masterly reliefs of Mayan priests flank the main stairway.

The perfection of the architecture in Palenque is made even more fascinating by the profusion of stucco reliefs. Not only are these found on the walls, cornices and pilasters of the palace, but they once decorated the roof combs as well. These certainly rank among the finest works of Mayan art and are also the most humanly expressive and alive sculptures of all ancient America. This also applies to the stucco heads, apparently portraits, found in the burial-chamber of the Temple of Inscriptions. Without question they are as good as many ancient Egyptian carved heads. Unfortunately only a few of the rich stucco decorations on the pilasters of the Great Palace have survived. They suffered particularly severe damage from the fire which the early discoverers thoughtlessly started in order to clear the ruins of their dense undergrowth.

The four expeditions to Palenque led by the Mexican archaeologist Alberto Ruz Lhuillier in the fifties were especially successful. In 1952 he found the entrance to a crypt on the top platform of the Temple-Pyramid of Inscriptions. A stone slab concealed a tunnel with a steeply descending stairway. The rubble which filled the tunnel had to be laboriously removed before anyone could go down the steps. Eventually Alberto Ruz found himself before a heavy triangular stone door which turned on an axis and barred the way to the crypt. Once they had penetrated this, the archaeologists reached a room containing a stone sarcophagus. The top consisted of a slab of limestone carved with a relief weighing 8 tons. When they raised it they found the bones of a priest-king who had been laid to rest there by the Maya along with many valuable gifts of jade and other stones, and had not been disturbed since. To one side of the burial chamber stood an altar where the strange life-size stucco heads were found. These heads can now be seen together with the contents of the sarcophagus including the king's superb jade mask in the new Museo Nacional de Antropología in Mexico City.

This grave was one of the great discoveries of our century. Alberto Ruz says this about it: "Apart from the artistic and archaeological treasure which the secret chamber of the Temple of Inscriptions held, the discovery is valuable because it shows us that the pyramid served a double purpose: it bore the temple and it contained a sanctuary concealed from the common people where the most secret and important rites of the Mayan religion were celebrated, probably involving human sacrifices."

Relief-carving on the stone cover of the sarcophagus found in the burial-chamber of the Temple of Inscriptions in Palenque. In the middle is the picture of the young king

13   Sayil-Labná-Kabah

Between the 4th and 8th centuries the great city-states of the central zone like Palenque, Uaxactún, Tikal and Copán reached their apogee. At the same time similar city-states began to develop in the north of the peninsula of Yucatán, independently of the southern states at first, and with clearly different styles from them. The most important of these was the Puuc style. Since there are no dates on buildings and stelae in the North it is extremely difficult to determine exactly when individual buildings were erected, while in Palenque or Copán the most important buildings may have the year of their erection on them. However, we do know that the Puuc style and the styles of Río Bec and Chenes developed during the 7th and 9th centuries and that they first arose in the middle of the 6th century.

Puuc is the name of a chain of mountains running from Mérida through the peninsula in a south-westerly direction. Puuc means 'land of low hills'. These uplands consist of coarse limestone and also include clay-filled hollows. Because the white limestone is the predominant rock the Maya called this area *zahcab*, which means "white earth". In many places the limestone has been eroded away; here the soil assumes a reddish-yellow colour from the iron oxide with which it is compounded, and for this reason is called *kanchab*, or 'yellow earth'. The limestone is exceedingly porous, so that rain-water soaks away through it like a sieve until it reaches the underground levels of clay. Underground pools and rivers form on this layer of clay 26ft to 33ft below ground-level, but there are no rivers on the surface in Yucatán. In some place the underground pools are accessible where the ground has given way to form sink-holes. These are called *cenotes* in Spanish, which comes from the Maya word *tzonot*. Wherever the Maya found *cenotes* they built settlements and towns. In addition they built cisterns for water-storage, and if there was no *cenote* they constructed artificial underground lakes which were fed by rain-water. The Río Bec and Chenes styles occur mostly in the remote areas of the southern part of the Yucatán Peninsula. Even so, examples are not restricted to Hochob, but also appear in Uxmal and even in Chichén-Itzá, places which are otherwise thought of as centres of the Puuc style. The Río Bec style extends further southwards than the other Yucatán styles. Many buildings in this idiom resemble the tower-like structures on the pyramids of Tikal, while the Chenes style can be recognised by the use of masks as decoration which often cover the entire façade of a building. Decorative reliefs of the Río Bec style are based on the combination of the two techniques of stucco and stone mosaic.

Kukulkán, the plumed serpent of the Maya, was essentially the same as the Mexican Quetzalcoatl. There are a number of symbols included in the image of the god

While Mayan decoration in Palenque still consists mainly of arabesques and foliage patterns, in Yucatán it gives way to abstract forms. This was basically a result of the materials used. Easily workable stucco lends itself to light, graceful shapes and branching forms, while brittle limestone is better suited to mosaics and similar techniques which tend to produce geometric motifs like crosses, strips, cubes and squares. Since all three of the new styles in Yucatán use the same or similar techniques, it is often difficult to distinguish between them.

The Puuc style is the most clearly distinguishable from the others because buildings of this type have smooth walls with on ornate frieze at the top. In addition the strip of decoration is separated from the undecorated area by a broad moulding which continues right round the entire building. The Mexican archaeologists call this 'moldura de atadura'. This kind of decoration derives from imitation of the rope bindings used to secure the wooden structure of a straw-thatched hut. This process of so-called 'petrification' can be seen even more clearly in the rows of balustrades which are also typical of the Puuc style. These cylindrically-shaped stones set close together, such as can be seen at Sayil and Labná and on the Tortoise House in Uxmal, are obviously an imitation of palisade walls in stone.

The architecture of Sayil, Labná and Kabáh is all in the Puuc style.

To get to Sayil and Labná, one leaves the main road from Uxmal to Kabáh and goes down a path cut through the bush which is now usable for cross-country vehicles. There are remains of masonry hidden everywhere in the bush. You have to look carefully to find the traces of these remains in the dense evergreen undergrowth, but suddenly you see a temple standing completely alone in some thin woodland, which is called Xlampak. This quite unexpected sight can make a stronger impact than a well cleaned and restored temple.

The great palace in Sayil dominating the city site, which is one of the most beautiful of all Maya buildings, dates from the 8th or 9th century. At first glance the palace seems to be a three-storeyed building. In fact it is a sort of pyramid in three broad steps like terraces, and the chambers set back on these should not really be thought of as rooms, but rather as cloisters built round the centre of a pyramid. There is a broad stairway which divides the building into two halves. It was in very bad condition, but the east side of the ground floor has recently been restored with all its ornamentation. The lower part of the stairway has also been restored to its original state. The most richly decorated is the middle level. Wide entrance-ways supported by pillars have been arranged at harmonious intervals along the unusually long front. The upper level has less ornamentation and has a series of window-like openings placed at wide intervals. Although it is so massive and closed-in, the building still seems very light and elegant.

The frieze and stylised ornamentation projecting slightly from the plain walls are in pure Puuc style. This design, which is especially effective on the lower and upper levels of the Sayil palace, is also found in Uxmal and Chichén-Itzá. In Sayil and also in Labná there are a few mouldings consisting of rows of adjoining pilasters. In the middle section of the palace at Sayil even the façades between the doorways are decorated with pillars with richly carved profiles. These pillars show particularly clearly that this design is based on tree-trunks bound together with ropes. Even the three bulges of the rope fastenings were imitated in stone. The rope was needed for thatched huts to strengthen the palisade walls so they could take the pressure of the roof.

Quite often the Maya used wooden roof-beams for their palaces and temples. Of course the wood decayed comparatively quickly, which is one reason why so many of their buildings have collapsed inside. These beams were often decorated with artistic carvings. A few planks have been found at Tikal and Piedra Negras in really quite good condition.

Yuum Kaax, the young god of the corn

In Labná there are similar pillar decorations to the ones at Sayil on the so-called Triumphal Arch, a masterpiece of Mayan architecture. The decorations combine dove-tailed balustrades and large spiral patterns.

The Triumphal Arch is a rarity in Mayan architecture. As the Maya cities of this time were not fortified and had no walls, they needed no gates. When the Mayans erected a monumental gate it was generally part of a complex of buildings such as in the Nuns' House and the so-called Dove-House in Uxmal. However, archaeologists do actually call the great Gate of Labná, which formerly linked two parts of the city, a triumphal arch.

The renovation of this marvellous building was begun in 1927. It has now been finished, and must be considered particularly successful. The richest design is on the western façade. On each side of the arch is a chamber with an entrance at the middle. As usual with the Puuc style, the lower part of the wall was left plain and the ornamentation only starts above a projecting moulding. There is also another example of how the Maya were influenced by the old wooden architecture in the forms they employed. Just above each entrance we find a *choza* or straw-thatched house realistically imitated in stone. These chozas are flanked on each side by pierced stone panels.

The presumption that the Gate of Labná and the other free-standing arches in the Maya region are really triumphal arches, and the archaeologists can give us no other explanation, makes another structure more comprehensible, namely,

Itzamná the 'learning god' or the 'wise god' is always shown as an old man. As the 'god of the heavens' he is one of the chief gods of the Maya

the impressive Arch of Kabáh. This monument stands on the edge of the city of Kabáh at the start of a ten-mile paved Mayan road, which in places is still in very good condition. It resembles a triumphal arch of the Roman Empire, with the road leading up to the arch in an absolutely straight line from quite a considerable distance. Everything seems calculated to create a grandiose and solemn impression. Even though the Mayans had no horses or chariots, they still had many solemn processions which were marked by a great deal of pomp.

The robes and trappings of the Mayan high dignitaries were just as splendid as the wealth of decoration on their buildings. The many portrayals in reliefs and above all the marvellous wall-paintings of Bonampak provide us with an attractive picture of all the details of ornaments worn for festivals and of the splendid processions themselves. We can well imagine what a Mayan ruler must have looked like as he made his entry through the great gate towering above the city, wearing a truly monumental headdress consisting of the mask of the Rain God and a basket-work support holding countless shimmering Quetzal feathers which were often taller than the wearer himself.

Kabáh was one of the most extensive Maya settlements of northern Yucatán and a source of many finds for the archaeologist. But here too, as with most of the ruined sites, it has up to non only been possible to deal with the most impor-

Wandering Mayan traders and boat-traffic along the coast of Yucatán. A wall-painting inside the Warrior Temple at Chichén-Itzá which no longer exists

tant buildings, chiefly the Codz-Pop or Palace of Masks. This buildings is 152ft long and 20ft high. Its name does not come from the builders, but was given to it in later times because of the enormous number of masks of the Rain God super-imposed on the entire front of the palace. Originally there must have been about 250 stone masks each consisting of 30 separate parts. The façade has been partly restored to its original appearance, but there are still hundreds of scattered fragments lying around. These have actually been sorted out, and one day every stone will be put back in its proper place.

The stone masks of the Rain God Chac with their great round sunken eyes and the S-shaped trunks protruding from them are probably based on designs taken from wood-carvings.

The dry peninsula of Yucatán has very much less rain than Petén or the Usumacinta Basin. Water is often scarce, and so it is understandable that the Rain God should enjoy a specially privileged position. We can see how impor-tant he was to the Maya from the large number of masks collected together on this temple. The mask of the Rain God becomes a leitmotiv in itself in Puuc style decoration, so that it is not only found on temples dedicated to the Rain God, but also on many other buildings particularly in Uxmal and Chichén-Itzá. The stylised masks of the 'Codz-Pop' of Kabáh derive from the Puuc style while the variety of the ornamentation reaching right to the ground comes from the Chenes style. The richness of the design of this strange building is the result of a fusion of styles. This palace is another masterpiece of Maya architecture.

Relief pictures on the frieze of the inner temple of the Sooth-Sayer Pyramid at Uxmal ▷

14   Uxmal

Maya culture in Yucatán flourished between the 9th and 11th century A.D. The Toltecs reached the peninsula between the year 1000 and 1200. This is now known for certain. In spite of this there remain a number of questions which are still unclear, above all concerning the mysterious appearance of Quetzalcoatl. Was this a historical fact or does it belong entirely to myth?

One thing we do know is that the arrival of the Toltecs was marked by a tremendous resurgence in Mayan architecture and a real renaissance began. Naturally, a city like Uxmal did not grow up overnight; in fact it is probably the oldest Maya city in Yucatán. Over the centuries there was a great deal of rebuilding and alteration, and there are some elements of decoration which show signs of Toltec influence, but the city was probably never under Toltec occupation.

Uxmal is one of the most impressive city-sites in the northern part of the Maya region. This could already be seen from the drawings Catherwood made in 1841. These became very useful as a guide in 1928 when the Mexican Ministry of Education authorised the beginning of the city's reconstruction. Over a period

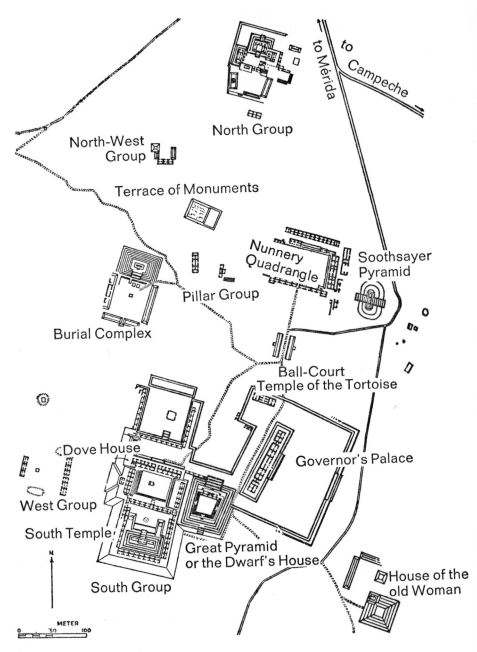

to Mérida

to Campeche

North Group

North-West Group

Terrace of Monuments

Nunnery Quadrangle

Soothsayer Pyramid

Pillar Group

Burial Complex

Ball-Court
Temple of the Tortoise

Dove House

Governor's Palace

West Group

South Temple

Great Pyramid
or the Dwarf's House

House of the
old Woman

South Group

N

METER
0   50   100

Plan of the ruins of Uxmal

of ten years the most important buildings were rebuilt with outstanding success. These now stand before us in all their old former splendour, though others which are equally deserving still wait to be rebuilt. They include the Dove House, which gets its name from decorations resembling dove-cotes, the South Temple, the Pyramid of the Old Woman, and the ball-court.

The temple-area of Uxmal stretches over a wide plateau with a strange building 125ft high, the so-called Sooth-Sayer Pyramid towering over it. The classical pyramid form has been abandoned here. It is as if the Mayan architects had remembered the mountain peaks where the gods had been worshipped in the hazy past.

The Sooth-Sayer Pyramid is oval in plan. It contains five pyramids which were covered over during repeated rebuildings. The entire process of construction probably extended over three centuries before it reached its final form. A very steep stairway of 150 steps leads up to the summit, on which stands the last of the five temples. The other four temples lie underneath this one, one inside the other. All five temples have survived. Temple 4 has the richest decorations, including an ante-chamber in Chenes style with masks of the Rain God. This motif is also found on the other temples, and there is an ornamental strip on both sides of the steep stairway with a continuous series of masks of the Rain God Chac. We can be fairly sure that this building was a temple to the Rain God.

The Governor's Palace is built in pure Puuc style. Like all the important buildings in Uxmal, this architectural masterpiece stands isolated on the grounds, which occupy an area of about 250 acres. It stands on a hill rising 50ft above this space which is flattened at the top to make a platform. The building has a rather

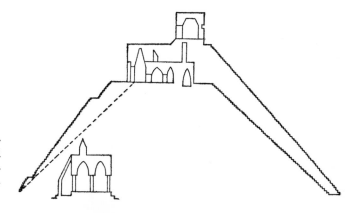

Cross-section of the Sooth-Sayer Pyramid in Uxmal showing how it was rebuilt. Temple 3 is in Chenes style

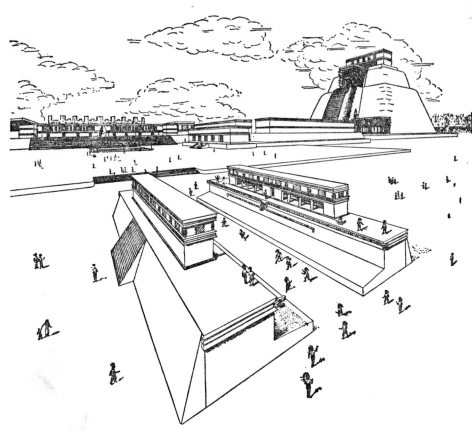

Reconstruction of the buildings of Uxmal

sophisticated design, with its façade set back in two stages and a 10ft high mosaic frieze making a strong contrast to the smooth, undecorated walls with their 11 doorways. Almost 20,000 dressed stones, each weighing between 55 and 175 pounds, were used in this mosaic frieze. 150 masks of the Rain God and 10,000 Saint Andrew's crosses have been counted among the motifs.

The so-called Nunnery Quadrangle is generally thought to be one of the most magnificent complexes of buildings in Uxmal. Like all the buildings in Uxmal it is built of white coral limestone. It consists of four groups of edifices surrounding a squared courtyard. The façades facing on to the courtyard are richly decorated with mosaics, like the façade of the the Governor's Palace. Above the geometric pattern there are many naturalistically portrayed figures, such as a plumed serpent with human face looking out of its open mouth, a throne with a canopy and sculptures of human forms. On the frieze of the west wing there are also imitations of straw-thatched huts carved in stone.

The name Nunnery comes from the Spaniards of the colonial period and is certainly wrong. There were in fact maidens in the temple-cities of Yucatán whose lives were devoted to religious duties. It was their task to tend the temple fires. (It has been conjectured that in Chichén-Itzá at certain times maidens were sacrificed to the Rain God by being thrown alive and dressed in their full regalia into the sacred *cenote*, a huge sink-hole where the water-level was 66ft below ground level.) However, it is most unlikely that this large complex of buildings with 88 rooms was occupied solely by these 'nuns'. It may have been a palace for the rulers or some kind of school for priests, with the appropriate accommodation for ceremonial. Nevertheless, the name Nunnery has been kept because it is so widely accepted.

The name Tortoise Temple is very simple and unproblematic. This building got its name from the carvings of tortoises on the top cornice. On the other hand Uxmal is a Mayan name. It means in the Mayan language 'built three times'. According to legend, the Sooth-Sayer's Pyramid (also known as the Magician's Pyramid) was built by a hunch-backed dwarf, who was also a magician, in three nights. This might explain its name too.

The Spaniards were probably right in most cases when they called many of the larger buildings *palacios*. These structures with their many chambers often arranged in two or three rows one behind the other are real palaces in our sense of the word, and were certainly built as such.

Kukulkán, the plumed serpent god,
on a relief in Chichén-Itzá

15 Chichén-Itzá

While Uxmal is completely unified in character, apart from a few exceptional
examples of Chenes style, Chichén-Itzá has two faces. The buildings of the
early period are in the Puuc style, but those from later times show features which
are not pure Mayan, and are the result of Toltec occupation.

An inscription in the classical Mayan picture-numerals found on the thresh-
hold of a decaying building on the south side of Chichén-Itzá gives a date eqiva-
lent to the year A.D. 618. This is the earliest recorded date to have come down
to us in the city. The great cities of the south, Tikal, Copán and Palenque, were
still flourishing at this time, but there had already been a great deal of building
going on in the north, in Yucatán. Although 618 is the earliest written date, there
is no evidence that this was the first building to be put up in the city.

Many scholars, such as Walter Lehmann, believe that Mexican influences in the
peninsula of Yucatán can be traced back to long before the birth of Christ.
Artistic skills and knowledge passed down along the Maya roads, which were
maintained from early times, not only to Petén and the Usumacinta Basin, but
even as far as Yucatán, where Mayan communities were already living.

When the Toltecs advanced into Yucatán in about the year A.D. 1000, as
invading warriors rather than peaceful craftsmen as in former times they
conquered the Maya and adopted their language. They introduced new gods
into the religion and completely reconstructed Chichén-Itzá in the style of
Tollán, their former home. It reached a new stage of intellectual and cultural
development after the Mayan cities outside Yucatán had mysteriously fallen
into decline.

Around the year 1200, when Toltec power in mainland Mexico had waned,
Chichén was suddenly abandoned by the Toltecs. In the second quarter of the
13th century, a group of Maya from Campeche, who called themselves Itzá,
wandered into Yucatán. They took over the deserted capital and gave it its

present name, Chichén-Itzá ("the mouth of the well of the Itzá", a reference to the sacred *cenote).* Later they founded another city not far away called Mayapán.

Mayapán was taken over in 1283 by an Itzá family, the Cocom, who then ruled the whole of Yucatán. Since there were no longer any religious ties, which up to that time had been the spur to all religious building, construction in the cities was much reduced and art began to decline.

The second half of the fifteenth century saw the rise of the Xiu tribe. They destroyed the city of Mayapán – massacring the Cocom – succeeded in driving the Itzá out of Chichén, and tried to conquer the entire country. This attempt failed, but more and more tribes rose up and quarrelled amongst themselves. When the Spaniards arrived here they found merely the remnants of the Maya nation which had once made such outstanding achievements in art and learning.

The arrival of the war-like Toltecs marked the beginning of the epoch of fusion among the cultures of this region. Two races met here and two different traditions in art confronted one another. Gradually the Toltec tradition gained more and more ground. It expressed itself most powerfully in the use of the column, and the column became a major motif in the architecture of Chichén-Itzá. It was the greatest idea ever to enrich the skills of Maya builders. The best example of this is the well-known Temple of the Warriors. This is almost square in plan, and so similar in design to the 'Temple of the Morning Star' at Tula that one could almost take it for a copy.

In both places there is an ante-chamber in front of the stepped pyramid with its broad stairway. This introduced a method of supporting roofs which was entirely new to the Maya. Until then they had only been able to build roofs over narrow corridors using the technique of the false arch. Now, with the column, it was possible to build roofs over rooms as wide as they were long.

The pillars of the adjacent Northern Colonnade consisted of several sections placed one on top of the other, and these supported a roof made of square stone slabs resting on wooden beams. Over the centuries the wood rotted away and collapsed. When the beams gave way they brought the whole building down with them. The columns have now been sorted out of the rubble with a great deal of labour and set up again, but the stone roofing has not been reconstructed.

As at Tula, the entrance to the Warriors is flanked by two serpent-pillars. Their heads lie on the ground with gaping jaws, and their bodies stand in vertical position while the ends of their tails are curved, thus serving both as decoration and as support for the architrave.

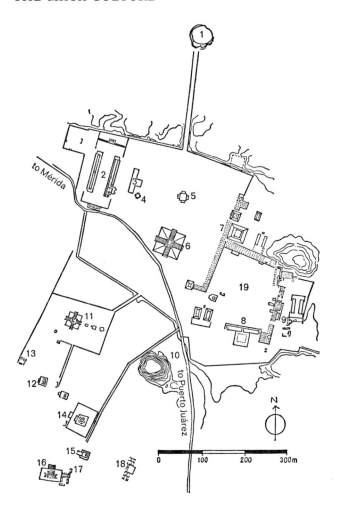

Plan of the ruins of
Chichén-Itzá

1 Sacred cenote	11 Tomb of the Great Priest
2 Ball-court with Temple of the Jaguars	12 La Casa Colorada (The Coloured House)
3 Tzompantli	13 La Casa del Venado (The House of the Stag)
4 Platform of Tigers and Eagles	14 El Caracol Observatory
5 Platform of Venus	15 Temple of Decorated Plaques
6 El Castillo (Pyramid of Kukulkán)	16 The Nuns' House and associated buildings
7 Warriors' Temple	17 La Iglesia (The church)
8 Market place	18 El Akab – Dzib
9 Steam bath	19 Group of the 'Thousand Pillars'
10 Cenote and temple of Xtoloc	

Fortunately this city, abandoned by its inhabitants, was not destroyed by the Spanish. Neither was it used as a stone-quarry, as happened to so many ruined sites. Only nature destroyed this work of man. It was half a millennium before archaeologists began to take an interest in this city again, after it became the property of the United States' consul in Mérida, Edward H. Thompson, in the 1880's. Thompson was as enthusiastic about ancient Mayan cities as John Stephens had been, and he purchased the whole stretch of land where Chichén-Itzá lay – such things were still possible in his day – so that we could devote himself to his hobby undisturbed. This meant above all exploring the sacred *cenote*.

Everything was more or less complete at Chichén-Itzá except that most of the buildings had collapsed, and the confused mass of stones had been engulfed by the bush. Nevertheless, there was still enough of it standing for most of buildings to be reconstructed without too much trouble. It just needed time, a lot of money and tireless labour. This great task was undertaken by the Carnegie Foundation together with the Mexican Institute of Education. This enabled the scholars led by Sylvanus G. Morley, the founding father of Mayan studies, after 20 years of work to turn the great ruined city into a really beautiful open-air museum.

The 78ft high main pyramid standing in the middle of the city is popularly known as El Castillo. It rises above a base 180ft square in nine steps as a symbolic image of the heavens in the mythical world of the ancient Mexicans. On each side a flight of 91 steps leads up to the platform at the top, so that the total number of steps adds up to 364. Counting the platform as on step the total is 365, equal to the number of days in a year. Each side of the pyramid is in addition faced with 52 stone slabs, which is the same as the number of years in the calendar cycle of the sun year.

On the platform at the top of the pyramid stands the Temple of Kukulkán. Its broad doorway is divided into two by a pair of serpent-columns. When the archaeologists began to reconstruct this pyramid, they discovered a perfectly preserved temple right at the heart of it, standing on a smaller pyramid which was completely superimposed by a later temple. Today the inner chamber of this temple can be reached through a long gallery. It is still in exactly the condition it was in when the priests abandoned it about 1000 years ago at the time of rebuilding. Its Chac Mool and the red-painted stone jaguar with its surface picked out with 73 inlaid jade fragments have survived undamaged.

The Chac Mool is a figure which is half lying and half sitting up. On its stomach it has a hollow or dish carved out of the stone where religious offerings were probably put. It is not quite clear exacly who it represents. Some people believe it to be the image of a pulque-god, and others think he was the messenger who carried offerings to the gods. The name Chac-Mool is a combination of Chac, the Rain God, and Mool, the jaguar. It was coined by Le Plongeon, who carried out some excavations at Chichén-Itzá in the eighties and found one of these strange sculptures.

The Caracol is a particularly interesting building, the only round structure in Chichén-Itzá. The name has nothing to do with its purpose. It means 'snail-shell', and comes from the spiral stairway inside the building which resembles a snail-shell. This was the city's observatory. The Caracol is the oldest building in the Toltec style. It was erected on a series of terraces. When it was rebuilt on the last occasion another platform was added to the top terrace, so that the tower now seems to have sunk down several feet into it. At the top there is a small chamber equipped with sighting holes set out for astronomical observations.

A monumental building from the Mexican epoch stands opposite the Castillo on the great square. This is the Temple of the Jaguars, another tower-like building, which contains two temples. The lower one opens on to the great empty square, while the upper one is a raised temple reached by a steep open stairway. There is a free-standing sculpture of a jaguar at the entrance to the lower temple which was the altar. The opening at the other end faces on to the ball-court, and is flanked by two serpent-columns like the entrance to the Temple of Warriors.

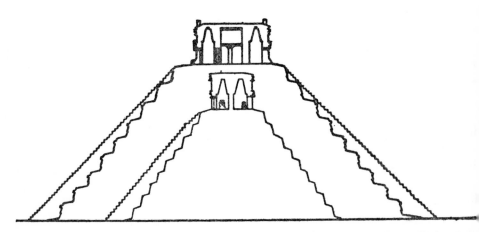

The stages of rebuilding of the great pyramid of Kukulkán, known as the Castillo, at Chichén-Itzá

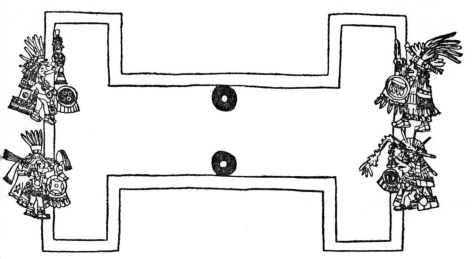

Ball-court of the gods. Quetzalcoatl and Coatlicue (on the right) are playing with Xochipilli and Ixtililton

The ball-court directly adjoins the Jaguar Temple, that is one of the walls between which the game took place is at the same time one of the long walls of the temple. Since the ball game was a religious rite among all the peoples of ancient Mexico, it is not surprising that temples were often built very close to the ball-courts. The size of ball-courts and the arrangement of the walls varies from city to city. What they all have in common is the basic shape of a double 'T' or an 'H' stretched out sideways. Most of the Mayan courts have sloping walls round them with a pitch of less than 40 degrees. The one at Chichén-Itzá is built in the Toltec way and has high vertical wall 272ft long. They were constructed with massive square stone blocks to a height of 27ft. The playing area, or *rachtli*-field, between them is 199ft wide. A heavy stone ring projects at right angles from the mid-point of each side-wall 23ft from the ground. These are decorated with reliefs of snake-designs.

Two small temples dedicated to the Sun and Moon Gods mark the ends of the arena.

The H-shaped plan of the ball-court is a symbol of the four cardinal compass directions. The earthly ball-game represents the cosmic ball-game of the gods, for it was believed that they were playing ball with the sun and moon as they followed their course through the firmament.

As the game was a religious act it could only be played by members of the priestly caste. The heavy hard rubber ball had to go through the stone rings, and it could only be struck with the knee, elbow or hip. These were the fundamental rules of the game, but there were also variations from place to place.

Relief on a wall of the ball-court at Chichén-Itzá. The two sides stand facing one another. The kneeling player has just had his head cut off by the winner standing opposite him. A fountain of blood shoots out of his neck. The winner is holding the defeated player's head in one hand and an obsidian knife in the other. The picture gives a clear idea of the cruelty involved in the Toltec ball-game

On the Mexican Plateau the game was presided over by its own special god. This was Xolotl, the god with the double form. But other gods liked to amuse themselves by playing this game with the heavenly bodies, as the mythology of the Maya and Aztecs describes. Quetzalcoatl as the Wind God would play with the God of Health, Ixtlilton, and with Xochipilli-Cinteotl, for example. The God of Young Maize chose an old woman for his partner, the goddess Cihuacoatl-Ilamatecuhtli.

Perhaps the sacred ball-game of the Maya and other cultured peoples of Middle America was based on a similar idea to the Olympic Games of the Greeks, since these were also dedicated to the gods. In any case the people of ancient American high cultures saw our earthly existence as a small reflection of the eternal and limitless macrocosm of the gods.

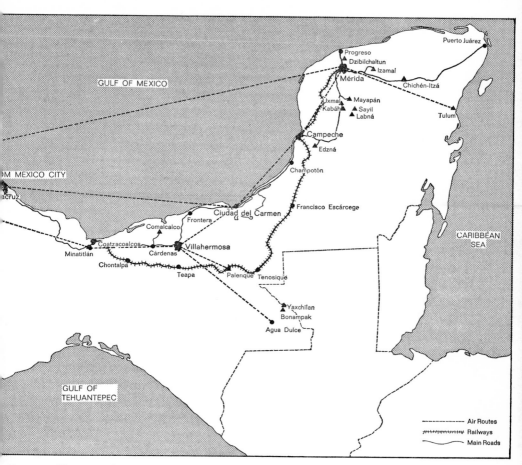

Routes to Yucatán and the Mayan sites

Advice on Travelling in Mexico

Mexico has an excellent network of roads which has been considerably extended and improved in recent years to that all the archaeological sites described in this book can be easily reached. For travelling from one archaeological zone to another the distances are often long enough to make it worth going by aeroplane.

Only a few major sites can be reached by railway, among them Palenque. However, now that the Pan-American Highway is open, it is much quicker by road as the railway makes a long detour over Veracruz.

In 1952 a new line was opened in Mexico, the Línea del Ferrocarril del Sureste, primarily intended to carry hardwoods felled in the jungle. It is 457 miles long and links Coatzacoalcos and Campeche, and also passes Palenque. In the fifties there was still no road from the Central Mexican Plateau to Yucatán so one had to use this line. The section from Coatzacoalcos to Campeche, which was missing, has now been built, though it fellows a different route from the railway and passes through Minatitlán and Villahermosa.

The railways to Teotihuacán, Tula and Toluca are now rarely used by tourists. They are old and slow. Most prefer to take the bus.

Cuicuilco lies on the same solidified lava-field, the Pedregal, as the Ciudad Universitaria, the new university. It is on the very outskirts of Mexico City in the Distrito Federal. The Insurgentes Sur leads directly into the Ciudad Universitaria and the road then continues in the direction of Tlalpan. The pyramid stands to the left of the road just before Tlalpan.

Teotihuacán is also easily reached by motor-road. A bus leaves about every half hour for Teotihuacán. Those who would prefer a guided tour should apply to any travel agency in Mexico. This also applies to other excursions in the vicinity of the city. The advantages and disadvantages of these parties are well known to everybody. Entry into the archaeological area of Teotihuacán is allowed between 8 a.m. and 6 p.m., and is free on Sundays. A small entrance fee is charged on weekdays. The newly-built museum is open from 10 a.m. until 4.20 p.m.

The distance by road from Mexico City to the pyramids is 32 miles. You take the road marked Laredo out of the city. It branches off at Venta de Carpio towards San Juan de Teotihuacán passing the famous Acolman Monastery on the way, so it is possible to combine a look at this interesting building from the colonial period with the visit to Teotihuacán.

Tula is in the state of Hidalgo about 50 miles north of the capital and can be reached by car and rail. Both the railway and road pass the famous Tajo de Nochistongo dam at Huehuetoca (29 miles). It is 4¹/₂ miles long built in colonial times to protect the capital from flooding in the rainy season, which is what often happened.

The majority of tourists prefer the road to rail travel. You leave the city on the new road heading north, the Avenida M. Ávila Camacho. This goes through the satellite city of Satélite direct to Tula. However, it is a good idea to make a detour on the homeward journey to Actopan, a wonderful Augustinian monastery from the 16th century which stands just off the road to Laredo 74 miles from Mexico City. The town of Tula with 8000 inhabitants also has an interesting church and a 16th century convent. In many of the old houses in the town prehistoric stones and sculptures were used as building material, and we also know that after Tollán was destroyed in A.D. 1168 the Aztecs took many of the sculptures to their own capital, Tenochtitlán. The archaeological area of Tula is very close to the town.

Tenayuca is only 6 miles north-west of the capital. You drive down the Insurgentes as far as the Monumento a la Raza. You then take the Calzada Vallejo which branches off here and leads directly to Tenayuca.

Santa Cecilia is only 2 miles from Tenayuca. The well restored Aztec pyramid stands in the middle of the village.

Calixtlahuaca lies on the Plateau of Toluca and is the only archaeological site in this large region which has been studied and restored. It can only be reached from Toluca. Toluca is 40 miles from Mexcio City and is linked by a road and railway line, but here again it is better to go by car than take a train. The Federal Highway 15 in the direction of Guadalajara leads to Toluca, which has one of the largest and most interesting Indian markets in Mexico, best visited on Fridays. From Toluca you take the Querétaro road for 7 miles until a road forks left for Calixtlahuaca. The archaeological area lies on the left side of the Río Tejalpa.

Malinalco can also be reached by bus via Toluca. However it is not a good idea to try and visit Calixtlahuaca and Malinalco on the same day, as there would not really be enough time for both and the journey is quite tiring. There is a direct bus link between Mexico City and Malinalco. The bus first goes to Toluca on the same road as for the trip to Calixtlahuaca. The road then turns off at Toluca and goes via Tenancingo and Ixtapan de la Sal to Taxco. A short distance before Tenancingo, 72 miles from Mexico City, an unpaved road turns off to the left, passing through a fertile valley and then along the Montes del Mixtongo as far as the heights of Matlalac (5800ft). It then goes steeply downhill to Malinalco, a little town nestling between mountains. The ruins lie above this place at the so-called Cerro de los Ídolos, which is reached along a steep footpath.

Xochicalco is 25 miles from Cuernavaca and lies 360ft above a broad plain on a spur of the volcano Ajusco. One can get to Cuernavaca from Mexico City by bus on the new or old trunk road, but there is no bus connection to Xochicalco. You can continue the journey in a private car or with an excursion organised by a travel agency, first taking the road towards Taxco. A road to the Cacahuamilpa Caves leads off this at Alpuyeca (62 miles). You go down this for 200 yards to where another road turns off. This is a good road, and continues to Xochicalco 2¹/₂ miles away.

La Venta, the most important site where Olmec large-scale sculptures have been found, and which gave its name to one of the cultures of the Gulf Coast, lies in the middle of the jungle and is very difficult to reach. It is probably not worth making the trip to La Venta as all the important stone monuments have been removed and set up in the Parque Museo de La Venta at Villahermosa. These finds are extremely interesting, so it is well worth visiting the open-air museum. The remarkable monuments have been arranged here in their natural environment just as they were found 60 miles away in the north of the state of Tabasco. The Parque Museo de La Venta is situated very close to Villahermosa airport. It is also a good idea to visit the Museo de Tabasco in the town, for here are displayed superb examples of objects from La Venta.

Since Villahermosa is not only accessible by aeroplane, but also lies on the route of the new trunk road from Mexico to Yucatán, a visit here can easily be combined with a journey to Yucatán.

The objects found at Tres Zapotes and Cerro de las Mesas, including a few gigantic Olmec stone heads, are exhibited in the museum park of Jalapa in the same way as at Villahermosa. Jalapa is on the highway linking Veracruz and Puebla.

El Tajín, 200 miles from Mexico City, can be reached on an excellent road via

Pachuca, Tulancingo, Huachinango, and Poza Rica. The return journey can be made via Papantla and Jalapa. This will bring the total distance to 318 miles.

El Tajín is 5 miles south of Papantla and about the same distance from the large oil-refining centre of Poza Rica. It is also possible to take an aeroplane from Mexico City to Poza Rica.

Monte Albán, set 1300ft above the Valley of Oaxaca, is easily accessible from the provincial capital, Oaxaca. Oaxaca is on the Pan-American Road and is 375 miles from Mexico City. It is better not to try and take in Monte Albán and Mitla on the same day. The regional archaeological museum of Oaxaca should not be missed. One can see some of the gold objects found in Grave 7 at Monte Albán displayed there behind unbreakable glass.

To reach Monte Albán, drive down the Calle de Carlos Mariá Bustamente from the main plaza in a southerly direction and then turn right into the Calle de Arista. At the Calle de 20 Novembre take the same street to the left, cross the Río Atoyac and then go straight to the archaeological area of Monte Albán.

Mitla is 31 miles south-west of Oaxaca. First we take the Pan-American Road towards Tehuantepec. After a little less than 25 miles a road leads off direct to Mitla. Before one gets to Tlacolula it is a good idea to take a side-road to the small village of Santa María del Tule. In the grave-yard in front of the church stands the famous Tree of Tule described by Alexander von Humboldt. This tree is an Ahuehuetl or 'water spirit' and thought to date from the 15th century. Its mighty trunk is 40 yards in circumference.

Yagul is the third archaeological area in the Valley of Oaxaca where systematic studies and excavations have been made. Yagul lies 1/2 mile from the Pan-American Road, and if you have a car, you can combine this with a visit to Mitla. An un-tarred road leads from Tlacolula, but this is hardly usable in the rainy season.

Yagul is a town in the same style, and probably built at the same time, as Mitla. The excavations here are not yet finished. The town is divided into two sections. In the lower part stand the temple and palaces, while on the hill rising above it there is a fortress whose marvellous design is easily recognised.

Palenque lies on a north-west spur of the Sierra de Chiapas, on the borders of South Campeche and Tabasco. This well-wooded plain forms the rainiest part of Mexico. The archaeological site of Palenque is 5 miles away from the town of Santo Domingo de Palenque and the railway station on the Coatzacoalcos-Campeche line. As there are only a small number of trains of the Ferrocarril del Sureste every week and the 110 mile journey by automobile can be very tiring, especially in the rainy season, most people prefer to take a plane here from Villahermosa. The Compañía Tabasqueña de Aviación runs a service of small twin-engined aircraft carrying from 5 to 9 passengers. Arrangements for a flight can be made at the airfield in Villahermosa. Planes operated by the same company also fly to Bonampak. The landing-strip at Bonampak can only be used in good weather conditions, so it is possible to land there and then a few hours later not be able to take off again, and for this reason there is always a certain amount of risk involved in a trip there. It is also possible to reach Bonampak overland, but it needs the equipment for a real expedition. Nevertheless, the splendid murals in vivid colors will indubitably repay the visitor for his trouble.

The best thing to do when visiting the Mayan cities of Yucatán is to make Mérida one's base. It is now only 1 1/2 hours away from Mexico City by jet.

Kabáh and *Uxmal* are on the trunk road between Mérida and Campeche. If the tourist comes from Mexico in his own car, he can visit the ruins of Edzná along a side-road from Campeche, and he can visit Kabáh and Uxmal before getting to Mérida. If he takes the plane to Mérida, he can hire a taxi for a day-trip to Uxmal.

There are two very good tourist hotels at Uxmal, but they are not cheap, and are mostly booked up. It is advisable to book a room in plenty of time beforehand through a travel agency. Of course, one can also quite easily go to Uxmal and Kabáh with an organised tour.

Labná and *Sayil* are best reached by jeep or a cross-country vehicle. These can be obtained through a travel agency in Mérida and will be held ready at Uxmal or Kabáh.

You leave Kabáh on a rough track through the bush. It takes 2 hours to reach Labná and its famous triumphal arch, and then on the way to Sayil you pass a building half smothered by the jungle, which is the temple of *Xlampak,* and an ancient water reservoir with stucco figures of doves and women bathing.

You leave Sayil by a different road which joins the main road between Uxmal and Kabáh.

Chichén-Itzá is 75 miles from Mérida on an extremely good road linking Mérida with Valladolid and Puerto Juárez. There is a good hotel in Chichén-

Itzá too, and the same points apply here as to the hotels at Uxmal. It is worth spending 2 or 3 days here for anyone really interested in the large archaeological site of this Mayan city, but one day is enough to form a good general impression. In this case it is best to visit the northern part of the city, with the Pyramid of Kukulkán and the Warriors' Temple, in the morning, and the southern part, with the Caracol, in the afternoon.

It is also possible to make day-trips from Mérida to other sites, especially *Mayapán* and *Dzibilchaltún,* a huge area of ruins where excavations are still going on.

Tulum on the other hand is more difficult to reach. This important Maya temple-city from the later period lies 25 miles from the island of Cozumel on the east coast of Yucatán in the state of Quintana Roo. There is a regular air service to Cozumel, which has ideal conditions for swimming and underwater sport. An excursion to Tulum can be arranged by motor-boat. There are also small light aircraft which may be chartered in Mérida for direct flights to Tulum.

The god over the door of the Temple of the Descending God in Tulum

The name 'Tulum' means wall or fortress, and dates from recent times. The original name was probably Zamá, as ancient chronicles record that there was a city of that name on the east coast of Yucatán at the time of the Spanish conquest. Zamá means 'sunrise', and Zamá lies on that part of the Yucatán coast where the sun does actually rise.

Dzibilchaltún was almost completely destroyed, but there are still quite a few important buildings which have survived at Tulum. The most impressive of these is the Castillo, a well preserved temple-pyramid in the centre of the city. The buildings of the ceremonial area are enclosed by a city-wall measuring 420 yards from north to south and 180 yards from west to east. Since Tulum stands right by the sea, the cliffs form the boundary on one side.

The Temple of the Hanging God is another interesting building. It acquires its name from a stucco sculpture in a niche above the entrance. Very beautiful frescoes have survived in one of the temples. Stephens and Catherwood were the first explorers to visit Tulum (1842). Later on Howe and Morley also made a study of Tulum, and the Carnegie Foundation in Washington organised three expeditions there in the years 1916 to 1922. The results of these were later published by Lothrop.

A road is planned which will go from Tulum via Cobá, another important archaeological site, to the main Mérida – Puerto Juárez road, but at the moment no usable road to Tulum exists.

Everyone who is interested in the ancient culture of this country should visit the *Museo Nacional de Antropología* in Mexico City, if possible, before they go to the various archaeological sites of Mexico.

The work of building this museum was begun in 1960. It is in the park of Chapúltepec on the Paseo de la Reforma covering an area of 150,000 square yards, and is considered one of the largest and most important museums of the world. Architects, historians, archaeologists and ethnologists all worked together to produce something remarkable both for its outward appearance and its contents. Although most of the objects displayed are real works of art, the museum is not a 'museo de arte', but a 'museo de historia'. It is intended first and foremost to show the public the development and historical relationships of the great prehistoric cultures by means of magnificent examples of archaeological finds, models, dioramas, plans and photographs.

Even the site of the museum on the edge of the marvellous Chapúltepec Park, which is where the Aztecs settled after their long years of wandering, is strange and remarkable. One crosses a large courtyard to get to the vestibule, and inside there is a row of models which give information about the arrangement of the various cultural areas using written descriptions which light up automatically, and an automatic system of tape-recordings. One then reaches the vast inner court. In the middle of this stands a huge concrete mushroom with a surface 4,800 square yards in area. Water streams down from this surface in a constant

A mighty stone figure of Tlaloc stands guard in front of the Museo Nacional de Antropología in Mexico City

105 The gigantic concrete mushroom underneath which there is a constant 'rain'. The water disappear
the stone floor

106 The inner-court of the museum with the concrete mushroom which covers an area of about 5000 square yards

107 A stone symbol of the huge Aztec skull-racks

108 26 inch high ceremonial censer with a mask and crown of feathers, from Teotihuacán

109 Animal-shaped pottery vessel decorated with sea-shells, from Teotihuacán

110 Clay vessels in human form from Teotihuacán

111   A Zapotec burial-urn made of pottery, representing the Zapotec rain-god Cocijo

Zapotec burial-urn in the form of a jaguar from Monte Albán

113   Aztec stone sculptures of the earth-goddess Coatlicue

stream like rain, but instead of falling into a pool it disappears through fine holes in the concrete floor.

The exhibition halls grouped round this inner court have displays representing every important culture of ancient Mexico. The wing on the right as one comes in from the vestibule is devoted to the great cultures of the Mexican Plateau, the Archaic Period, Teotihuacán, the Toltecs and Aztecs. The left wing is concerned with the cultures of the Maya, the Gulf Coast, Oaxaca and the west and north of Mexico. The objects are arranged chronologically, each series ending with the period leading up to the ethnography of our own time. The exhibition rooms for the ethnographic regions are on the second floor directly above the particular cultures whose regions are still occupied by Indian tribes today.

On the left of the vestibule there is a stall where the most important publications on archaeology and ethnology can be obtained.

The museum also includes the following departments: a school offering graduate courses in ethnology, physical anthropology, linguistics and archaeology, a library of 250,000 volumes, a reading room which is open to the public, and an archive of historical documents and a collection of microfilms.

Most material collected in archaeological research is first of all assembled in this building. These collections are the source of material for all the other museums which the Instituto Nacional de Antropología supports in many other states of the country.

The museum is open from Monday to Friday between 10 a.m. and 2 p.m. and from 4 p.m. to 8 p.m. On Saturdays, Sundays and public holidays it is open right through from 10 a.m. until 6 p.m.

Bibliography

Frans Blom and O. La Farge, *Tribes and Temple* , 2 vols, New Orleans, 1926

George W. Brainerd, *The Maya Civilisation*, Los Angeles, Calif., 1954

A. Caso, *The Aztecs*, Norman, Okla., 1968

Michael D. Coe, *The Maya*, London/New York, 1966

———, *Mexico*, London/New York, 1962

Miguel Covarrubias, *Indian Art of Mexico and Central America*, New York, 1957

Miguel Covarrubias, *Mexico South*, New York, 1956

P. Dark, *Mixtec Ethnohistory, A Method of Analysis of the Codical Art*, Oxford/New York, 1958

William H. Holmes, *Archaeological Studies Among the Ancient Cities of Mexico*, 2 vols., Chicago, 1895–97

Alfred Kidder II and C.S. Chinchilla, *The Art of the Ancient Maya*, New York, 1959

E. Kingsborough, *Antiquities of Mexico*, London, 1831

G. Kubler, *The Art and Architecture of Ancient America*, Harmondsworth/Baltimore, 1962

S. Linné, *Archaeological Researches at Teotihuacan*, Stockholm, 1934

S. Linné, *Zapotecan Antiquities*, Stockholm, 1938

S.K. Lothrop, *Pre-Columbian Art*, New York, 1957

Sylvanus G. Morley, *The Ancient Maya*, 3d. rev. ed., Stanford, Calif, 1956

Frederick A. Peterson, *Ancient Mexico*, New York, 1959

H.E.D. Pollock, et al, *Mayapan, Yucatan, Mexico*, Washington D.C., 1962

William H. Prescott, *The Conquest of Mexico*, 2 vols., London/New York, 1957

Donald Robertson, *Pre-Columbian Architecture*, New York, 1963

R.L. Roys, *The Political Georgraphy of the Yucatan Maya*, Washington D.C., 1957

T. Proskouriakoff. *An Album of Maya Architecture*, Washington D.C., 1946

T. Proskouriakoff, *A Study of Classic Maya Sculpture*, Washington D.C., 1950

Karl Ruppert et al, *Bonampak, Chiapas, Mexico*, Washington D.C., 1955

The South American Handbook, London/Chicago annually (for comprehensive travel information on Mexico, etc.)

John L. Stephens, *Incidents of Travel in Central America, Chiapas and Yucatan* (drawings by Catherwood), New Brunswick, N.J., 1949

J.E.S. Thompson, *Maya Hieroglyphic Writing*, Washington D.C., 1950

J.E.S. Thompson, *Mexico Before Cortez . . .*, London/New York, 1933

G. Vaillant, *The Aztecs of Mexico*, Harmondsworth/Baltimore, 1950

V.W. von Hagen, *The Ancient Sun Kingdoms of the Americas . . . Aztec, Maya, Inca*, London, 1967

V.W. von Hagen, *The Aztec: Man and Tribe*, New York, 1958

V.W. von Hagen, *World of the Maya*, New York, 1964

The *Official Guides* to major sites, published by the Instituto Nacional de Antropología e Historia, Córdoba, 43, 45 and 47, México D.F

Index

Acolman, San Agustín 162
Acosta, J. R. 40
Actopan, San Agustín 163
Alzate y Ramírez, José Antonio 50
Arch ("false") 135f., 153
Archaic cultures 12ff., 17, 46, 55f., 177
Astronomical observatory
  at Chichén-Itzá 81, 156; Ills. 98-100, 103
  at Mayapán 81
  at Monte Albán 73
  at Palenque 81, 137; Ill. 55
  at Uaxactún 81
Atlantes 9, 40, 42; Ills. 6, 8
Axayacatl 46
Aztecs 7f., 16f., 20, 37ff., 43ff., 54ff., 74, 79, 163,
  168, 177; Ills. 5, 14-25, 107, 113

Ball-court 157
  at Chichén-Itzá 156f.; Ills. 92, 93
  at Copán 52, 73
  at El Tajín 66
  at Monte Albán 73
  at Uxmal 149
  at Xochicalco 50, 52; Ill. 23
  Mayan 157
  Toltec 157
Ball-game 68, 157f.
Blom, Frans 134
Bonampak 144, 166
Burgoa, Francisco de 77

Cacahuamilpa Caves 164
Calendar 9, 37, 44, 66, 81
  Aztec 44, 52
  Mayan 81ff., 155
Calixtlahuaca 46f., 163; Ills. 18, 19
Campeche 133, 152, 162, 165f.
Carnegie Foundation 155, 168
Caso, Alfonso 73f.
Catherwood, Frederick 133, 147, 168
Ce Acatl Topiltzin 42
Cenotes 84, 140, 151, 153, 155; Ill. 96
Cerro de las Mesas 54ff., 164
Chac-Mool 155f.; Ill. 13
Chapúltepec Park 168
Charnay, Désiré 77
Chenes style 84, 140, 146, 149, 152; Ill. 73
Chiapas 81, 133
Chichén-Itzá 12, 81, 84, 140, 142, 145f., 151, 152ff.,
  166ff.; Ills. 86-103
  Ball-court 156f.; Ills. 92, 93
  Caracol (Observatory) 81, 156, 167; Ills. 98-100, 103
  Castillo (Temple of Kukulkán) 155f., 167; Ill. 86
  Northern Colonnade 153
  Nunnery Ills. 101, 102
  Platform of Tigers and Eagles Ill. 91
  Temple of the Jaguars 156f.; Ills. 89-92
  Temple of the Warriors 45, 153, 156, 167; Ills. 87, 88
  Tomb of the Great Priest Ill. 97
Chichimecs 42, 44
Cholula 20, 75
  Pyramid 20
City planning 7ff.
  at Monte Albán 71ff.
  at Palenque 136f.
  at Tenayuca 44
  at Teotihuacán 20
  at Tula 40
Clavigero, Francisco J. 49

Coatzacoalcos 133, 162
Cobá 168
Cocom 153
Copán 52, 73, 140, 152
Copilco 15
Cortés, Hernando 43, 45
Cozumel 167
Cranial deformation 67
Cuernavaca 50, 164
Cuicuilco, Pyramid of 14f., 162; Ills. 1, 2

Danzantes 73f.; Ills. 38, 39, 43
Diodorus Siculus 78
Dzibilchaltún 83, 167f.

Edzná 166
Etla 70

Gods 8f., 18, 37, 39, 67, 82, 156ff.
  Chac 145, 149, 156
  Cihuacoatl-Ilamatecuhtli 158
  Coatlicue 157; Ills. 5, 113
  Cocijo 74
  »Fat god« 38
  Fire god 20, 37f.
  Huitzilopochtli 44
  Itzamná 144
  Ixtlilton 157f.
  Jaguar god 56, 74
  Kukulkán 84, 141, 152, 156
  Maize god 158
  Moon god 157
  Quetzalcoatl 8, 37f., 40, 42f., 46, 84, 141, 147, 157f.;
    Ill. 8
  Rain god (see also Tlaloc, Chac) 18, 52, 84, 145f.,
    149f.
  Sun god 40, 52, 157
  Tepeyolotl 49, 56
  Tezcatlipoca 43, 45, 49
  Tlahuizcalpantecuhtli 40
  Tlaloc 19, 38, 44; Ill. 104
  Water god 20, 38
  Water goddess 20
  Wind god 46f.
  Xochipilli 157f.
  Xolotl 158
  Yuum Kaax 143
Guatemala 17, 79, 81, 133
Guatemala City 18

Hieroglyphs
  Aztec 45, 52, 73 f.
  Mayan 73f., 81
  Zapotec 71, 73f., Ill. 41
Hochob 140
Holmes, William H. 77
Honduras 79, 81, 133
Howe, George P. 168
Huastecs 54, 81
Huehuetoca, Tajo de Nochistongo dam 163
Human sacrifice 39f., 44, 47, 66f., 84, 139, 151
Humboldt, Alexander von 50, 77, 133, 165

Incidents of Travel in Central America, Chiapas and
  Yucatán (Stephens) 133
Indian market, Toluca 163
Instituto Nacional de Antropología e Historia 9, 177
Itzá 152f.

Jalapa 56, 164f.

Kabáh 140ff., 166; Ills. 71-73
  Arch 143f.; Ill. 71
  Codz-Pop (Palace of Masks) 145f.; Ills. 72, 73
Kaminaljuyú 18
Krickeberg, Walter 15, 38

INDEX

La Venta 54ff., 74, 164
Labná 8, 140ff., 166; *Ills.* 68–70
    Gate (Triumphal Arch) 8, 143, 166; *Ills.* 68, 69
    Temple of Statues *Ills.* 69, 70
Le Plongeon, Augustus 156
Lehmann, Walter 152

Malinalco 48f., 56, 163f.; *Ill.* 20
Manuscripts
    Aztec 49
    Mayan 74
    Mixtec 75
Matlatzincas 46
Maya 8, 18, 42, 50, 52, 56, 65ff., 70, 73f., 77, 79ff.,
    167, 177; *Ills.* 53-103
    area 81, 133
    foreign contact 42, 70, 74, 81, 84, 147, 152
    language 81, 84
Mayapán 81, 153, 167
Mérida 140, 155, 166ff.
Mexico City 12ff., 18, 43, 137, 162ff., 166, 168
Mictlan 75
Minatitlán 162
Mitla 70, 75ff., 165; *Ills.* 47-52
    Palace of Pillars 75, 77f.; *Ills.* 48, 50
Mixcoatl 39
Mixtec-Puebla culture 75
Mixtecs 50, 71, 73ff., 77; *Ills.* 47-52
Monte Albán 7, 17, 50, 70ff., 75, 77, 165; *Ills.* 38-46, 112
    Acropolis 73
    Ball-court 73
    North Platform 73; *Ill.* 40
    Observatory 73
    Tomb No. 7 73, 75, 165
Morley, Sylvanus G. 83, 155, 168
Museums (*see also* Open-air museums)
    Mexico City, Museo Nacional de Antropología 137,
    168f.; *Ills.* 104-113
    Teotihuacán, Museum 162
    Villahermosa, Museo de Tabasco 164

Nahuatl 15, 40, 50
Numeration 73f., 82f., 152; *Ill.* 41

Oaxaca 70ff., 75, 165, 177
Olmecs 54ff., 65f., 70, 73f., 81, 164; *Ills.* 26-31
Open-air museums
    at Chichén-Itzá 155
    at Jalapa 56, 164; *Ills.* 26, 29-31
    at Villahermosa 55f., 164; *Ills.* 27, 28
Otomí 46

Palenque 81, 133ff., 140f., 152, 162, 165f.; *Ills.* 53-60
    Great Palace 137; *Ills.* 55, 56
    Observatory 137
    Sun Temple 136; *Ill.* 53
    Temple of the Cross 136; *Ill.* 53
    Temple of the Foliated Cross 136; *Ill.* 54
    Temple of Inscriptions 136ff.; *Ill.* 60
Papantla 65, 165
Petén 81, 84, 145, 152
Piedras Negras 142
Poza Rica 65, 165
Puuc style 84, 140ff., 145f., 149, 152; *Ills.* 62-68, 83

Radiocarbon (carbon-14) dating 13, 17, 55
Remojadas style *Ills.* 35, 36
Río Bec style 84, 140
Roof construction techniques
    Mayan 135f., 143
    Tajín 67, 135
Ruz Lhuillier, Alberto 136f., 139

Sahagún, Bernardino de 17
Salvador 79
San Juan de Teotihuacán 162

Santa Cecilia, pyramid at 43, 45, 163; *Ill.* 17
Santo Domingo de Palenque 166
Sayil 140ff., 166; *Ills.* 62-67
    Palace 142; *Ills.* 62, 64
Seler, Eduard 77
Smithsonian Institution 55
Spaniards 8, 16, 54, 71, 75, 151, 153, 155
Stephens, John L. 133f., 155, 168
Stierlin, Henri 84
Stirling, M. W. 55

Tajín 54, 65ff., 135, 164f.; *Ills.* 32-37
    Ball-court 66
    Great Tajín (Niche Pyramid) 65f.; *Ills.* 32, 34
    Pillar Building 66f.
    Tajín Chico 66; *Ill.* 34
    Tunnel House 66
    West Court 66
Taxco 164
Tenayuca 43ff., 163; *Ills.* 14-16
    Pyramid 44f.; *Ills.* 14, 16
Tenochtitlán 8, 43ff., 49, 163
Teotihuacán 8, 12, 16ff., 39f., 44, 50, 52, 54, 65, 71,
    136f., 162, 177; *Ills.* 3, 4, 108-10
    "Citadel" 20, 38; *Ill.* 3
    Palace of Quetzalpapalotl 38
    Pyramid of the Moon 8, 18, 20
    Pyramid of the Sun 8, 18, 20; *Ill.* 4
    Temple of Quetzalcoatl 8, 37f.
    Way of the Dead 20, 136
Tequixquiác 12
Tetzcotzingo 48
Thompson, Edward H. 155
Tikal 18, 140, 142, 152
Tlatilco 13
Tollán (*see* Tula)
Toltecs 8, 39ff., 46, 54, 75, 79, 84, 147, 152f., 156f.,
    177; *Ills.* 6-13
Toluca 48, 162ff.
Totonacs 65
Tres Zapotes 54ff., 164
Tula (Tollán) 8f., 39ff., 152f., 162f.; *Ills.* 6-13
    Coatepantli 40; *Ill.* 11
    Temple of the Morning Star 40, 153; *Ills.* 7, 10, 12
Tulum 167f.
    Temple of the Hanging God 168

Uaxactún 81, 140
Usumacinta Basin 84, 145, 152
Uxmal 140ff., 146ff., 152, 166ff.; *Ills.* 74-85
    Ball-court 149
    Dove House 143, 149
    Governor's Palace 149f.; *Ills.* 74, 75
    Nunnery Quadrangle 143, 150f.; *Ills.* 77, 79-83
    Pyramid of the Old Woman 149
    Sooth-Sayer Pyramid 146, 149, 151; *Ills.* 76, 78, 79
    South Temple 149
    Tortoise Temple 141, 151

Villahermosa 55, 162, 164, 166

Warrior orders, Aztec 48f.

Xiu 153
Xiuhcoatl ("fire serpents") 45; *Ill.* 15
Xlampak 142, 166; *Ill.* 61
Xochicalco 7, 50ff., 164; *Ills.* 21-25
    Ball-court 50, 52; *Ill.* 23
    La Malinche pyramid 50ff.; *Ills.* 21, 22, 24, 25
Xoxo 70

Yagul 70, 165
Yucatán 9, 17, 42, 81, 83f., 133, 140f., 144f., 147,
    151f., 164, 166f.

Zapotecs 50, 65f., 70ff., 75, 78; *Ills.* 38-46, 111, 112